THE BOOK OF

endtimes

Also by John Clute

The Disinheriting Party

Strokes: Essays and Reviews 1966–1986

Look at the Evidence: Essays and Reviews

The Encyclopedia of Science Fiction (with Peter Nicholls)

Science Fiction: The Illustrated Encyclopedia

The Encyclopedia of Fantasy (with John Grant)

THE BOOK OF

endtimes

GRAPPLING WITH THE MILLENNIUM

by

JOHN CLUTE

HarperPrism
A Division of HarperCollinsPublishers

Since this page cannot legibly accommodate all the copyright notices,

pages 239-240 constitute an extension of this copyright page.

HarperPrism

A Division of HarperCollins*Publishers*

10 East 53rd Street, New York, NY 10022–5299

Copyright © 1999 by John Clute. All rights reserved.

For information address HarperCollins Publishers Inc.,

10 East 53rd Street, New York, NY 10022–5299.

ISBN 0-06-105033-4

HarperCollins®, ®, and HarperPrism® are

trademarks of HarperCollins Publishers Inc.

HarperPrism books may be purchased for educational,

business, or sales promotional use.

For information please write: Special Markets Department,

HarperCollins Publishers Inc.,

10 East 53rd Street, New York, NY 10022–5299.

First printing: November 1999

Designed by Roger Gorman/Reiner NYC

Printed in the United States of America

Library of Congress Cataloging-in-Publication Data

Clute, John, 1940–
    The book of end times : grappling with the millennium / John
Clute. -- 1st ed.
        p.   cm.
    Includes bibliographical references (p.   ).
    ISBN 0-06-105033-4
    1. Twenty-first century--Forecasts. 2. Millennium.
3. Civilization, Western--Forecasting.   I. Title
CB161.C58 1999
303.49'09'05--dc21   99-16603
                                                      CIP

Visit HarperPrism on the World Wide Web at

www.harpercollins.com

99 00 01 02 03 10 9 8 7 6 5 4 3 2 1

for
Liz Hand
in at the birth

A book like this, which reflects upon current thoughts and current events, is in a way all acknowledgments.

Acknowledgments all the way down. So I thank everyone mentioned or borrowed from or talked about in these pages.

Personal thanks to Judith Clute, Candida Frith-Macdonald, William Gibson, Liz Hand, David Langford, John Urling Clark,

Fred Pfeil, and Jack Womack; and to John Silbersack and Caitlin Blasdell of HarperPrism, for nerves of steel.

Last Judgement (detail), Hans Memling

Contents

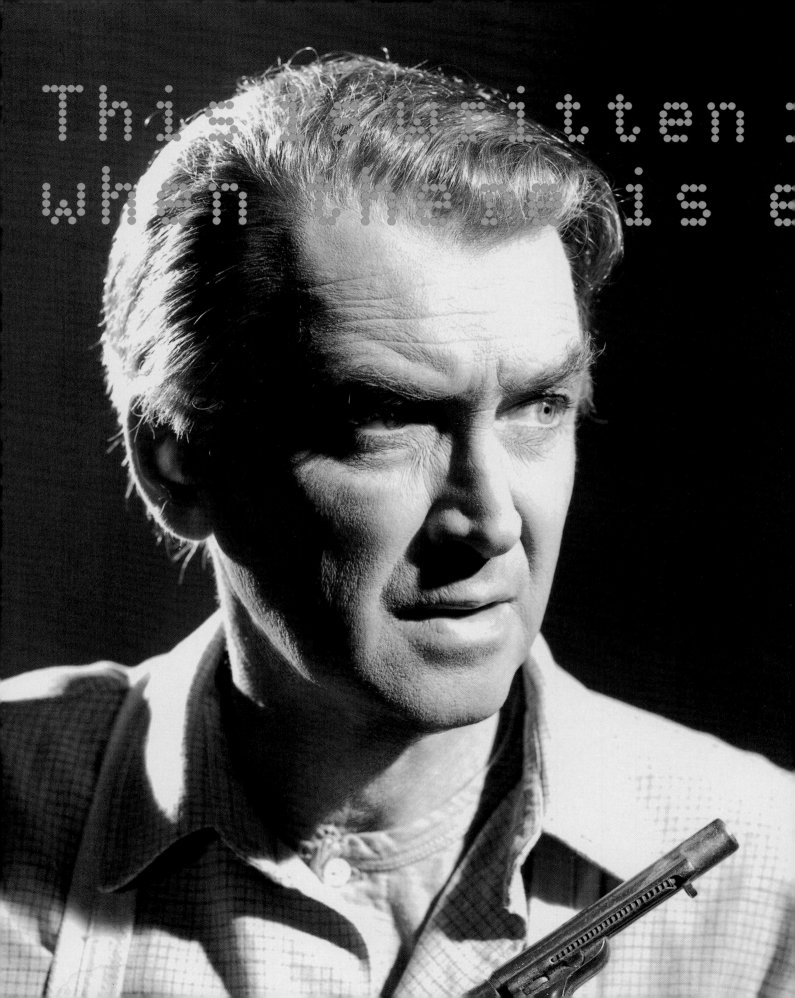

...n the dark days; ...vil in the air.

—SACHEVERELL SITWELL, *SACRED AND PROFANE LOVE*

But I told you when I began that I do not usually deal in the capital-*A* Apocalypse. What I've said so far has to do with the ongoing, the daily, the little-*a* apocalypse, and I believe that each of us today is aware, to some degree, of some convulsive quality in contemporary existence which may actually be new in the experience of the species. There are too many first times today, too many last times. These are the times, as the English writer Alan Moore has said, which we long for and dread.

—WILLIAM GIBSON

THE BOOK OF Prologue end times

It is the premise of this short book, this set of sketches in the shadows of the end, that millennium fever is nonsense, but that apocalypse is not. Whenever the advent of the Rough Beast Yeats imagined is calculated as a multiple of the figure 1,000, nonsense is uttered. But whenever it is suggested that the human race is approaching a turning point in its long and heavy-handed sovereignty over planet Earth—and that we do not yet know the nature of the new world to come—sense is being spoken.

The imminence of apocalypse rightfully seeds our dreams.

But there is a lot of nonsense being spoken right now.

In *The Book of End Times,* we hope to skirt the nonsense as much as possible, though we cannot avoid it entirely. Indeed, as 1999 swells toward 2000, and as the nonsense proliferates, and as the free-floating anxieties of the human race seek more and more desperately for irrelevant issues to focus on, it seems only fitting to produce a book about the end times that focuses on our diseased compulsion to misunderstand things, to be hysterical.

Definition
Hysteria:

From *hysterion,* which is Greek for "womb." A disease—often now called "conversion disorder"—where some scarring but inadmissible stress, which may be physical in origin but is usually psychic, surfaces as a symptom or symptoms seemingly unrelated to that original stress.

The Book of End Times **is all about hysteria.**

Above left: *The Garden of Earthly Delights* (detail), Hieronymus Bosch

The imminence
rightfully see

of apocalypse
is our dreams.

What a hysterical person does is always *something else*.

Fear of one thing is always acted out—converted into—fear of something else. As with the individual, so with the culture. Those in the Western world who fasten upon lame numerologies and incoherent anticipations of millennialism do so, in part, to avoid thinking in genuinely apocalyptic terms about the issues that rightly torment the thoughtful: the degradation of our home planet through overpopulation, global warming, turbulence of every sort; the almost infinite power of our technologies versus the archaic territoriality of our midbrains, which govern the nerves that pull the triggers of the godlike weapons we have crafted. In the Western world, then, today, the millennium is a hysteria of apocalypse.

Definitions

Apocalypse:

The imminent end of the present temporal world; in the Western world, this end tends to be a literal interpretation of the Book of Revelation.

Apocalypticism:

The belief that we are approaching the end of the present temporal world; in the Western world, this belief is often couched in Judeo-Christian terms.

Millennium:

A period of a thousand years. Originally it designated the period of Christ's rule on earth, as described in the Book of Revelation. More usually nowadays, it designates the *end* of a one-thousand-year period at (variously) midnight on 31 December 1999 or midnight on 31 December 2000. Other utterly precise points have also been designated.

Millennialism:

The belief in any of a huge number of predictions that the beginning of the year 2000 (or, variously, 2001) marks the end of the temporal world as we know it; the belief in any of a huge number of dire predictions about the world to come.

The Apocalyse (detail), Albrecht Dürer,

One by one the bulbs burned out, like long lives come to their expected ends. Then there was a dark house made once of time, made now of weather, and harder to find; impossible to find and not even as easy to

dream of as when it was alight. Stories last longer: but only by becoming only stories. It was anyway all a long time ago; the world, we know now, is as it is and not different; if there was ever a time when there were passages, doors, the borders open and many crossing, that time is not now. The world is older than it was. **Even the weather isn't as we remember it clearly once being;** never lately does there come a summer day such as we remember, never clouds as white as that, never grass as odorous or shade as deep and full of promise as we remember they can be, **as once upon a time they were.**

—JOHN CROWLEY, *LITTLE, BIG*

Apocalyptic literature and thought, grounded in fervent religious conviction, proclaims that a convulsion is due and that a massive shift is nearly upon us. Millennial literature and thought, building upon shaky arithmetical calculation, predicts the precise moment of the end.

In *The Book of End Times,* apocalyptic literature and thought are treated with respect—as a valid way to formulate specific apprehensions about the fate of the human race here and now, always keeping in mind the fact we have not yet established a living beachhead on any other planet. All the eggs of the race are in one basket.

The Book of End Times is divided into four sections.

Part One

provides a brief overview of the hysteria-ridden world of 1999, where we are now, and of how we fail to describe it to ourselves.

Part Two

offers some glimpses of how we behave here, how we behave as though we were not here at all.

Part Three

looks at some false prophets, at the dark mirror they hold to our faces, but recognizes that through that dark mirror it is possible to discern a Waste Land. Our anxieties, eternal and contemporary, are surely real and valid. There is a Waste Land, and it is all about us: The world outside our skins is burning up.

Part Four,

while making no predictions, suggests, very modestly, that we need a better tool than millennialism in order to grapple with the apocalypses within and without us.

So let us **begin.**

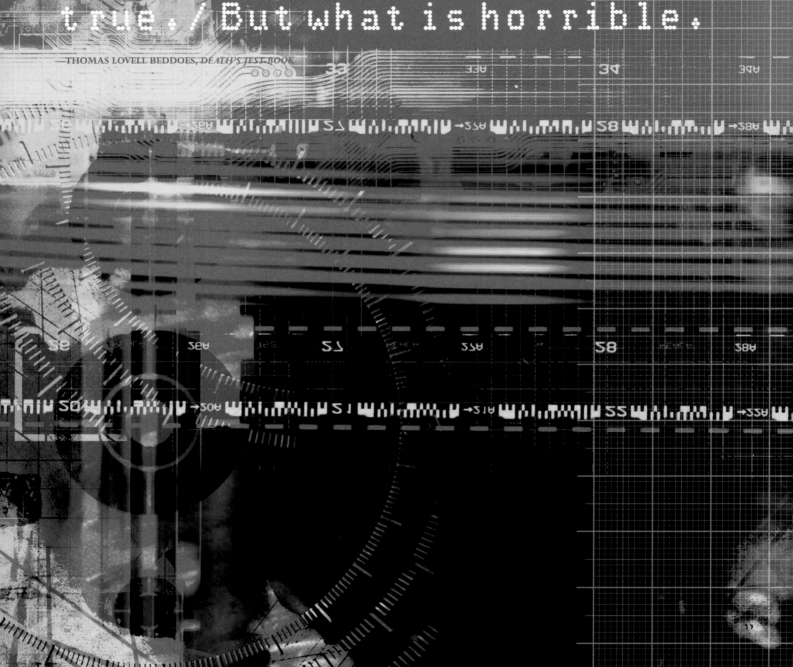

Methinks
The look of the world's a lie, a face made up / O'er graves and fiery depths; and nothing's true. / But what is horrible.

—THOMAS LOVELL BEDDOES, *DEATH'S JEST-BOOK*

A Story Called
Part One
millennium

I

THE END TIMES ARE US

It does not much matter where we start the end of time. So we can start now. It's 1999, and as we begin to close the books on the biggest century the human race has ever experienced, the Western world is beginning to swell like an egg, a very ripe egg about to hatch. Soon we will learn what it is we've been expecting. We have created the world to come in our dreams, through the extraordinary powers we now possess to shape the future of the world as though we were shaping a dream, and we are about to give birth to the year 2000. More than any year in history, the year 2000 is our creation. The year 2000 is our baby. What we do not know is whether or not it is going to be poisonous.

We are living in the middle of the end of time. Whether or not we pay conscious attention to the wishful thinking and rumor and speculation that has accumulated around the myth of the millennium,

O Judgment! thou are fled to brutish beasts,
And men have lost their reason.

—WILLIAM SHAKESPEARE, *JULIUS CAESAR*

something that looks like an ending shapes our dreams during these latter days. Its arrival is unlikely to be predicted through the use of the decimal system—even though a lot of computers may blow at the stroke of midnight on 1 January 2000, and the teeth of the world will rattle as a consequence—but we do know there's something in the air.

There is certainly the smell of our own fear as a species.

We want the world to be a sacred part of that long invention that is the story of our life, the most important character after ourselves. We yearn to live in a coherent place we can name, where we can feel safe inside our invention, and we want that place to exist like a friend, somebody we can know.

What we must understand is that we already inhabit such a place; it is alive. We must understand that the world cannot take care of itself anymore. The specific danger is us; this earth is our only friend, and we are destroying it increment by increment at a horrific rate.

We need to define a new and livable story; it will be a story about staying put and taking care of what we've got, in which our home is named as sacred, a story that encourages us to take serious care, a story about making use of the place where we live without killing it.

For we have told ourselves to be scared. But perhaps the scariest thing we should contemplate is that we of the twentieth century have the power to obey ourselves—the power to inflict our dreams upon the world—and that we have woven for ourselves the end times we are now entering, just as a caterpillar weaves its own cocoon. Whenever we think about it, whenever we think about the vast creaky edifice of millennial calculation—whether it be understood as a sense-making engine for the fearful and the believers, or as obscurant claptrap that distracts the more rational from a proper focus on dizzying moments ahead—we are telling a story

In the vast interweaving of stories by means of which we create and maintain our human cultures, the story of progress has been one of the deepest and most powerful. It appears and reappears in an infinite variety of guises. Stripped of any baggage, it is the simple idea that time has an arrow and that one end of the arrow is different from the other. Stories have beginnings and ends, actions have consequences. The entire structure of narrative depends upon this simple relationship. Implied in this way of thinking about the world is the idea that we are going somewhere, that the end of everything, like the end of a story, is going to be satisfying (otherwise by definition it isn't the end), that it will be in some sense definitive. That's what "end" *means,* with perhaps the sole exception of personal death; and we don't think about that much anyway. The invention of salvation—the idea that we're going *somewhere,* and that that somewhere has *intrinsic value*—must have been a hell of a kick. Among other things, it provided a structure of purpose, intention, reason; it's an immensely powerful idea, so powerful that it's become part of the epistemic wallpaper, still driving things along while being more or less invisible.

—ALLUCQUÈRE ROSANNE STONE

that we in the Western world have wrought together; it follows that whenever we talk about history coming to an end, and judgment being pronounced upon the world, we are also talking about being dead.

But hysterical conversion processes are always at work, and it is almost always the death of others we talk about.

Perhaps the deepest appeal of the millennium myth is that it says we will not die in the badlands to come in the next century, and that (as in a dream of omnipotent infancy) *nothing will change.* There will be no more loss. The millennium myth tells us that *we* will not change or die; it is a myth of salvation to those of us who pass muster, and a myth of damnation and scouring to explain the entirely visible degradation of the living planet.

Perhaps any story...

If the silent, half-conscious, intuitive faith of society could be fixed, it might possibly be found always tending towards belief in a future equilibrium of some sort, that should end in becoming stable; an idea which belongs to mechanics, and was probably the first idea that nature taught to a stone, or to an apple; to a lemur or an ape; before teaching it to Newton. Unfortunately for society, the physicists again abruptly interfere, like Sancho Panza's doctor, by earnest protests that, if one physical law exists more absolute than another, it is the law that stable equilibrium is death.

—HENRY ADAMS, *THE DEGRADATION OF THE DEMOCRATIC DOGMA*

...is better than none.

No. There is no perhaps about it.
Stories are the wind of time.

Not I, not I, but the wind that blows through me!

A fine wind is blowing the new direction of Time.

If only I let it bear me, carry me, if only it carry me!

If only I am sensitive, subtle, oh, delicate, a winged gift!

If only, most lovely of all, I yield myself and am borrowed

By the fine, fine wind that takes its course through the

chaos of the world

Like a fine, an exquisite chisel, a wedge-blade inserted;

If only I am keen and hard like the sheer tip of a wedge

Driven by invisible blows,

The rock will split, we shall come at the wonder, we shall

find the Hesperides.

Oh, for the wonder that bubbles into my soul,

I would be a good fountain, a good well-head,

Would blur no whisper, spoil no expression.

What is the knocking?

What is the knocking at the door in the night?

It is somebody wants to do us harm.

No, no, it is the three strange angels.

Admit them, admit them.

—D. H. LAWRENCE, "SONG OF A MAN WHO HAS COME THROUGH"

Hercules in the Garden of the Hesperides,
(detail), Antonio Pellegrini

There are many ways to approach an understanding of the state of mind we're in, but no easy single route to understanding. Those who try to define contemporary fears and anticipations about the year 2000 as being governed by the Revelation of St. John the Divine will not bring us very close to an understanding. As a series of usable anecdotes about Last Things, the Book of Revelation is an immensely valuable treasure trove; but as a principle of explanation, it is sadly defective. When we look at Revelation, we'll find that *as a story* it is very nearly nonsense.

The Revelation of St. John the Divine does not make sense.

Neither, of course, does the whole numerological farce of the millennium.

The engines of the end are spinning their wheels. Gravel! Gravel! Kitty litter!

—*THE LITTLE BOOK OF APHORISMS OF THE END*

But any story is better than none.

You can see it in the movies
And the paper and the tv news
Somebody's army is always on the move
There's going to be a battle
The lines have been drawn
They've got guns and tanks and planes
The wells have gone dry and the water is bad
And the air is acid rain

There's war after war and rumours of war
From the east
There's a rumbling in the ground
And they're talking about the Beast
Good mothers cry cause the rivers run high
With the blood of too many sons
Some people say peace is on the way
But the worst is still to come

Cause the prophets wrote about it
And Jesus spoke about it
And John got to take a look
And he told us what he saw
And it's easy to see
It's going by the Book

There's armies in the cities and the missiles
Stand ready for flying
A pale horse rides
    like the wind
Across the night
And that rumbling in the desert
Like thunder getting closer
Are the trumpets getting ready to blow
There's going to be shout that will wake the dead
We'd better be ready to go.

—CHESTER LESTER, *"GOIN' BY THE BOOK"*

There's flies in the kitchen

I can hear 'em there buzzing

And I ain't done nothing

Since I woke up today

How the hell can a person

Go to work in the morning

And come home in the evening

And have nothing to say

Make me an angel that flies from Montgomery

Make me a poster of an old rodeo

Just give me one thing that I can hold on to

To believe in this living is just a hard way to go

—JOHN PRINE, "ANGEL FROM MONTGOMERY"

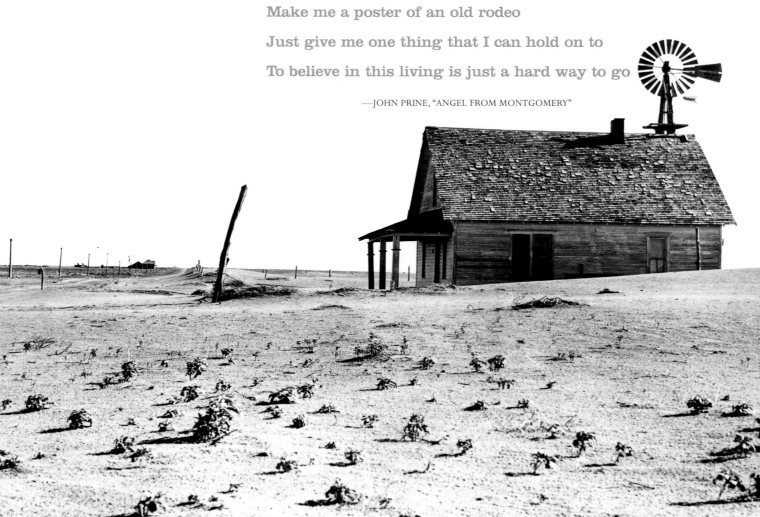

LIFE LINGERS ON

Let's take a look, for a moment, at no story at all.

Let's take a look at the fall 1997 special double issue of *Life* magazine, a journal whose growth and decline over the past half century mirrors America's own journey through the century, from the fresh beginnings through the heroic days of World War II and into the aftermath: the Cold War interstate Levittown Salk-vaccine baby-boomer junk-bond retrofix Internet years, all of us rich beyond the dreams of Croesus. It reads like one of those gossipy epics *Life* magazine in its prime specialized in bringing to America—but the days of glory, a time *Life*'s founder, Henry R. Luce, defined as "the American century" in 1941, and which reached its climax well before 1950, are long gone. The days Americans knew that America itself was a story, a story worth telling, are no longer with us. It is a story that *Life*, in its old age, has forgotten.

What the fall 1997 issue of *Life* does *not* resemble is the first issue of *Life* in 1950.

This 1997 special issue is one of many issued by *Life* and other journals of note as the century nears its end. We focus on it in particular because of *Life*'s long history as a voice of America, and because this magazine has always claimed that its rendering of the voice is particularly accurate. We focus on it because (up to a point) it tells us a story about who we are, how we got here, and where we're going.

The special issue in question is devoted to the most significant moments of the last thousand years in the shaping of Western history. During the period in question, a time most historians agree was increasingly dominated by the Western world, the history of the West is deemed by the editors of *Life* to be more or less identical to world history; and Western history, on a similar principle, ultimately becomes identical to the history of America.

The last thousand years, for the editors of *Life*,

have been a preparation for America.

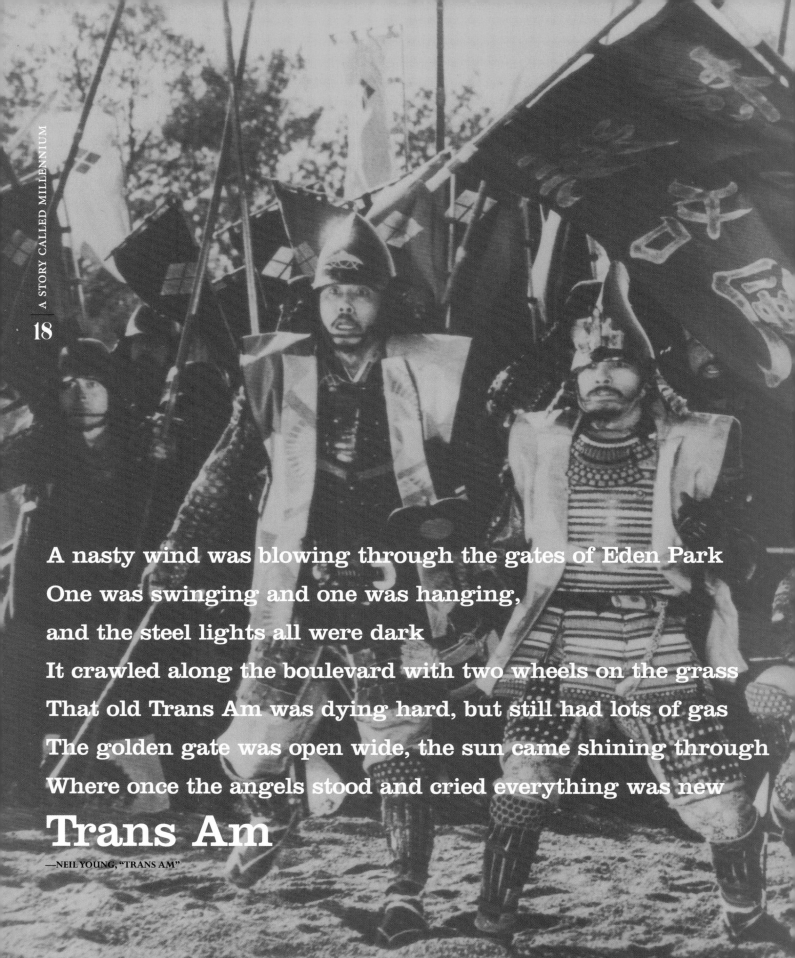

A nasty wind was blowing through the gates of Eden Park

One was swinging and one was hanging,
and the steel lights all were dark

It crawled along the boulevard with two wheels on the grass

That old Trans Am was dying hard, but still had lots of gas

The golden gate was open wide, the sun came shining through

Where once the angels stood and cried everything was new

Trans Am

—NEIL YOUNG, "TRANS AM"

For an America at the edge of Revelation?

Let us see.

There are five main sections of the *Life* special issue.

Part One briefly describes "the world as it was," focusing on the turn of the first millennium of the Christian era. It was a time "when some Europeans anticipated apocalypse. Pilgrims staged penitential processions; warriors swore oaths of peace to ecstatic crowds." And so on. But already we're in trouble. No real lesson about our own apocalyptic anxieties can be taken from this passage because, despite *Life*'s claims, there is considerable debate among historians as to whether or not any of this sort of description is actually true—and even if the description is (more or less) factual, there is absolutely no consensus on the significance of such scenes.

We can guess that the people of the year 1000 suffered,

When mankind shall again enjoy perfect health, when the soul and the body shall again be at peace with each other, one will hardly be able to understand the unnatural antagonism into which Christianity has plunged them.

—HEINRICH HEINE, *SCINTILLATIONS*

in some fashion, something that we might think of as apocalyptic anxieties; but it is almost certain that these feelings were not fixed into a millennial straitjacket. We don't know if people before 1000 A.D. behaved like preproduction models of how we might imagine ourselves behaving—though it's a pretty good guess that they behaved foolishly in their own way; and even if they did do certain things that *resemble* our own millennial fervors, we don't really know what they were thinking about when they did them.

Dark Ages indeed.

So there's little doubt that, in some but by no means all quarters, a certain apocalyptic anxiety was felt, but the supposed millenarian excesses at the close of the tenth century were an invention of medieval clerics centuries later.

The mental landscape of this particularly obscure period is particularly hard to pin down. But what the editors of *Life* are primarily interested in conveying is what one might call the "flavor of ago," a sight-and-sound bite of a time when folk, decently color-coded into their medieval roles, were humbly preparing to become *us.* Those agents of 1000 A.D. that we can no longer understand do not matter because *by definition* that which we cannot understand did not contribute to making us. That which we cannot comprehend is jetsam in the game of history.

So.

No help for us here.

There is nothing about 1000 A.D. that we can learn from *Life*.

The "petty kingdoms" of Europe, we are told, were just "emerging from darkness"—that is, from a region we cannot see. Nobles and "the nascent bourgeoisie were starting to take up reading," and fortunately (for us) "Arab scholars broke new ground," while Islam was "absorbing new ideas" from China. And so on and so forth. Gerunds—which make readers feel they have been taken to where the action is—are heavy on the ground. At the beginning of the year 1000, as we now begin to discover, there's a big story brewing. Out of that darkness we cannot understand begins the real story: the story of Europeans beginning to learn how to become more modern than before. A lot of world-historical scoops are about to explode in the faces of just-emerging-from-the-Dark-Ages folk. Let's hope they're up to becoming more like us.

The stage is set.

Let's continue. Part Two of this special issue is called "The 100 Events." It takes most of the remaining space. It lists in reverse order of importance those events deemed by two dozen editors of *Life*—who had "consulted scores of experts" in order to come up with a ranking—as being of primary importance in the story being told.

Some of this vast team's conclusions are, of course, controversial. It's odd, for instance, to find James Watson and Francis Crick's seminal discovery of the double helix shape of the DNA molecule ranked #76, just ahead of Elisha Graves Otis's demonstration of a safe elevator in 1854, but way behind the announcement of Robert Koch's germ theory of disease in 1882, which ranks #6, just behind Galileo's first sight of the moons of Jupiter.

As the massed editors of *Life* make smilingly clear, a ranking such as this is an arbitrary exercise, a kind of game. But even games that seem to have nothing to do with the outside world *always* have rules. The game being played here is a game of history. To play this game—its pieces include movers and nonmovers, shakers and nonshakers, neatly separated—we must have a particular *kind* of history in mind, one whose "rules" of significance or telling are transparent to the student or gamester; though there has never been a version of history without "rules," some versions hide them, while others allow them to preside visibly. Some versions emphasize "great" events;

Above right: *A Literary Research*, Lutwig Deutsch

Say to the children
of Daniel Boone:

Seek and you shall fine.
Rent and you shall rend.
Buy and you shall raze.
Breed and you shall bray.
Pay.

Things are mo re
now than they e

—DWIGHT D. EISENHOWER

some purport to decipher the real story of the world, which, though hidden to those who live it, is inevitable; some emphasize the daily lives of peasants; some rip aside the veils that have obscured women by redefining history as the story of what women immemorially do: care, share, shape, save the world (these are not guy things, and most histories of the world, being written by men and dealing with public events, effectively ignore them).

But every kind of history is, of course, a history of change—or there'd be nothing to tell. In any case, the editors of *Life* would never deny that they are interested in change. What they do *not* make clear is that the kind of change they're interested in is "rise." It is events and figures that contribute to the rise of the high-tech "modernized" world we now inhabit, the rise of the West, that grip their imaginations.

Unlike (for instance) women's history, the game of rise is a game of winners and losers, in which anything that contributes to rise is realer than the things that do not. It is the kind of history that emphasizes winners (those who are becoming like us), and in which the losers are missing a boat they did not know they were trying to catch; it is the history of progress. It is what has become known as Whig history, which Herbert Butterfield characterized in *The Whig Interpretation of History* (1931) as the kind of history that studies "the past with direct and perpetual reference to the present. Through this system of immediate reference to the present-day, historical personages can easily and irresistibly be classed into the men who furthered progress and the men who tried to hinder it." In American terms, it's probably the case that most historians (and orators) who speak of Manifest Destiny are recasting Whig history for a new continent.

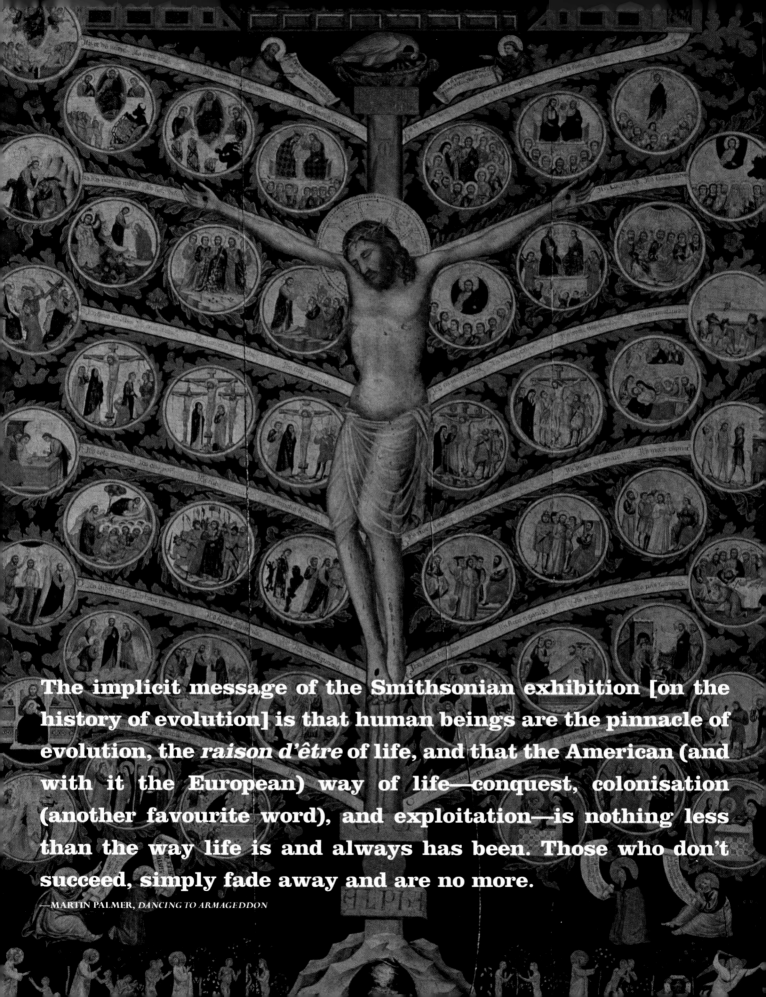

The implicit message of the Smithsonian exhibition [on the history of evolution] is that human beings are the pinnacle of evolution, the *raison d'être* of life, and that the American (and with it the European) way of life—conquest, colonisation (another favourite word), and exploitation—is nothing less than the way life is and always has been. Those who don't succeed, simply fade away and are no more.

—MARTIN PALMER, *DANCING TO ARMAGEDDON*

"Human history," as H. G. Wells put it in *The Outline of History* (1920), "is in essence a history of ideas." What he should have perhaps said, because this is what he was talking about, was that "a history of human progress is in essence a history of the ideas that win." History—Wells claimed then and *Life* magazine continues to claim now—is a game of rise where Johann Sebastian Bach may gain high marks for composing *The Well-Tempered Clavier* (it is ranked #43 in *Life*'s list) because it established equal temperament among keys for future generations to make use of. But Bach's greatest music, the cantatas and oratorios and the single great mass that together sum up and affirm an already existing world of faith, does not get a mention.

In other words, the story being told is the story of progress. The problem—one of many—with the story of progress is the same problem that mars a game, however amusing, that organizes chance and cards and boards and dice to shape a predetermined outcome. In a game, what is real is what wins. In the story of progress, what is real is what leads to us—or, dangerously, to a version of us simple enough to encapsulate in a hundred events. But what if winning the game of rise isn't really winning the real game of life? What if we need those Bach cantatas that don't get mentioned, and women's repetitive nurturing cycles, and the renewal of the worth of living every spring? Renewal and rise are different worlds.

The hope that man might control the course of events in harmony with spiritual values he has never yet attained is denied in the very momentum of history itself.

—RODERICK SEIDENBERG, *POST-HISTORIC MAN: AN INQUIRY*

A clue to what is being committed in this story of progress comes when we look at what happens when the one hundred most important events are presented not in reverse order of importance, as done in the special issue of *Life*, but chronologically.

Ironically—or perhaps inevitably, because it may have taken place a completely irrelevant year or so before the turn of the first millennium—the event deemed of greatest scientific importance by Richard Powers in a roughly similar special issue of *The New York Times Magazine*, 18 April 1999, does not get a mention in *Life*. This event—the demonstration by Ibn al-Haytham, or Alhazen, that light traveled to (not from) the eye—was of vital importance, not only because it solved a centuries-old dispute, but because Alhazen proved his case not through abstract argument but through observation. He asked observers to stare at the sun. If their eyes began to burn, it meant that light was entering them. **Their eyes began to burn.** Case proved.

But for most of the time span under consideration, the story holds, all right, and events for most of the period seem obedient enough. As we'd expect, not too much of significance happens in the first four centuries, from 1000 to 1399; some very telling moments—the earliest use of the nautical compass in 1117, at #10 (a good call), or Averroës's first translations of Aristotle in 1169, at #85 (pretty low, pretty low)—are duly included. But all in all, we have a sense that the main act of our story has not yet begun.

With the 1400s, the story starts in earnest. Gutenberg's development of a practical printing press in 1455 gets #1—*Life* is properly careful not to claim he actually invented an implement invented many times previously, the first printing press possibly being the one that imprinted images on a clay tablet found in Phaistos, Crete, and dating from around 1700 B.C.—and Columbus's opening of the West in 1492 gets #2. We are surely on the escalator of progress now.

The 1500s and the 1600s are chock-full, with twenty-one big ones. Some of them, such as the Industrial Revolution and Luther's invention of Protestantism, rank very high (#3 for Martin Luther), though some are weirdly undervalued, such as the defeat of the Spanish Armada in 1588, which eventually cost Spain her hegemony over both Europe and, eventually, America, and which is ranked #94, or the introduction of the Gregorian calendar, which tick-tocked Europe almost directly to the assembly line, ranked #100. But, as the editors of *Life* say, it's a game. Let's continue.

The 1700s are a dead ground: only six events of importance, three of those at the end of the century. Nothing much seems to have happened here—the invention of Romanticism (Goethe #0, Wordsworth #0) is of no more significance to the story of progress than the invention of classical music (Gluck #0, Mozart #0; Beethoven and Haydn, goose eggs both). But the doors are opening again.

The glorious century begins. From 1800 to 1899, no fewer than thirty-one events of world-historical rank are listed by the editors of *Life* and their scores of experts. Here Otis consorts with Singer (#67). Thomas Alva Edison (#11)—who in a separate section of the special issue is ranked the most important person of the last thousand years—gets a chance to improve Bell's telephone (#20). Water is filtered (#46); trains run (#24); refrigeration (#53) keeps food cold, except for canned food (#48), which doesn't need it; Coca-Cola (#82) is bottled. There are a few events of conventional history, too: Bolívar's liberation of Venezuela in 1821 (#74), for instance, though Bismarck's invention of the welfare state (#0) is referred to only under 1601, when the first poor law was enacted in England (#79). But, all in all, it's a stupendous century for events that change the physical circumstances under which we live—though of course, as is the almost invariable policy of the editors of *Life*, only those

events that, in their view, change things for the *good* are listed.

After all, history is about progress.
Isn't it?

The aborigines of Australia are losers, aren't they? So the year in which the last aborigine alive in Tasmania was killed by white settlers is not relevant.

The destruction of a people did not make us.

Did it?

The guilt of all the genocides of the last thousand years does not shape our dreams today.

Does it?

The bad things are irrelevant to our state of mind here in the West in 1999.

Aren't they?

We come to our own tumultuous, chock-full century. The editors of *Life* and their experts have found twenty-one events of importance here, though ten of them take place before the end of World War I. Einstein (#36)

Einstein spilled the beans.
—*THE LITTLE BOOK OF APHORISMS OF THE END*

gets a look in, but Niels Bohr's equally radical articulation of quantum theory is not deemed to be of world-historical heft.

More remarkable is that as the century continues, *Life*'s grasp of arguable world-historical events peters out very suddenly indeed. This may be due in part to focus; it's hard to assess the significance of events so close in time that their implications have not yet settled into consensus. Hard, maybe, but not impossible. Almost impossible, perhaps, but surely worth a try.

In any case, most of us have *more* ideas about the last half century than all the editors of *Life* together, plus experts. As far as this throng is concerned, the only world-historical events worth our attention after 1950 are the Crick and Watson double helix discovery, which they place way down in the rankings; Elvis Presley's laying down a cover of Big Boy Crudup's "That's All Right Mama" (#99); the publication in 1962 of Rachel Carson's *Silent Spring* (#70, which is a neat call); and the first moon landing (#33). And that's it.

Nothing since 1969 is worth noting, and of the four post–1950 items that *Life* does list, at least two are modestly dubious. Arguably as important for American music as Elvis's first recording was the 1951 release of Harry Smith's

If God did not exist, it would be necessary to invent him.

—VOLTAIRE, *LETTERS*

For within the hollow

That rounds the mortal temples of a kin

Keeps Death his cou

Above center: *The Trappers*, William T. Ranney

Anthology of American Folk Music for Folkways Records, a six-record set that brought America face-to-face with its own strange and enthralling musical past and deeply influenced almost every singer-songwriter (Elvis did not normally write his own music) in the generations since, including Bob Dylan, who I would argue is perhaps the most influential *creative* figure in American life over the past several decades, certainly as far as the vast baby-boomer generation is concerned, and who is not mentioned at all in the special issue. The *Anthology,* its sound cleaned up through digital remastering, was rereleased in 1997 by the Smithsonian, and began to influence a whole new generation. The songs collected here are amusing, pathetic, raunchy, surreal; many of them are dense with the very smell of apocalypse.

Is there a clue here?

There is no doubt that 1969's great moment, when *Homo sapiens* landed on the moon, is of symbolic importance (#33, to remind the forgetful)—but uniquely in *Life*'s special issue, the symbolism of the moon landing points not

rown

d there the antick sits,

Scoffing his state, and grinning at his pomp.

—WILLIAM SHAKESPEARE, *KING RICHARD THE SECOND*

forward but backward. It points to the end, not the beginning, of the story of the exploration of space in our century, for 1969 marks the end of that great Yankee story; it is the temporary end to a story that—if we survive the end of the century and the world-threatening events that apocalyptic anxieties license us to anticipate—will assuredly be told again, but in a very different guise, and not to us. As far as it goes, we who are adults today lost the story of space in 1969.

The world-historical space-related event that *Life* should have selected, because it concerned the future, not the past, is President Nixon's 1972 decision to shift the focus of NASA's efforts from the exploration and exploitation of the solar system in manned spaceships to the more "practical" development of a space shuttle. This closing down of the solar system for the men and women of the twentieth century was an event of utmost importance for every adult alive today—and ranks a lot higher than Otis's elevator in world-historical import.

The husk that is the space program of 1999 is a profound symbol of the inward-turning, self-scanning, frenetically retro spirit of our age. It reduces to nullity the great (if sometimes inflated) old story of how Yankee ingenuity and American willpower would make possible the penetration of new frontiers. It may seem strange to those of us alive now in 1999 and inundated in the end times cocoon, but the old Yankee story of the stars completely ignored the millennium; perhaps naively, it was a story that laid down an ever-unrolling scroll for Western civilization's upward course to the stars and beyond—that upward course whose significant moments the editors of *Life* so eagerly traced and glorified in this special issue, until of course the story ended in 1969. At this point the editors of *Life* fell silent, for they found themselves in a time they had no tale to explain. They had nothing to say about the invention of the transistor, or the Federal Aid Act of 1956 (which created the interstate highway system, the biggest artifact the world has ever seen), the polio vaccine, the birth control pill, the first geosynchronous satellite, the fall of the Berlin Wall, the collapse of the Soviet Union, the first unmistakable signs of global warming, the launch of the Hubble space telescope, the freeing (or unleashing) of information through the unrinsable anarchy of the Internet. They are as silent as President Nixon, they are as silent as the space we will never explore, they are as silent as the end of the world.

By denying space to us, in other words, President Nixon did something he was almost certainly unaware of. Against his own vision of the rise of America, and perhaps unconsciously, he did his best to undermine an understanding of the course of history that had dominated Western thought for several centuries and shaped the image of America as a land of Manifest Destiny.

Behold, then, rising now, as in the future, the empire which industry and self-government create. The growth of half a century, hewed out of the wilderness— its weapons, the axe and plough; the tactics, labor and energy; its soldiers, free and equal citizens. Behold the oracular goal to which our eagles march, and whither the phalanx of our States and people moves harmoniously on to plant a hundred States and consummate their civic greatness.
—WILLIAM GILPIN

He undermined America's image of history as a game of rise it was her Manifest Destiny to win.

President Nixon smashed the ladder of history.

More than a thousand incoherent "prophecies" of Nostradamus, more than Roswell, more than Waco, more than the massacre of two dozen children in a high school in the high-plains subtopia of suburban Denver, more than fears about not being year-2000-compliant, it is this smashing of Americans' belief that they were headed outward that has generated so powerful a sense that we have entered the end times—a period that may after all be best defined as the time that happens after real history has stopped. Simply by denying us (and the editors of *Life*) the old story,

President Nixon created a climate for apocalyptic thought. For a people used to first-class seats on the game of rise, the end times happen when history loses momentum.
The millennium—that is, the end of this century—is a vacuum we are now desperately trying to fill.

What is left, when there is no story, is not exactly the silence of the tomb, the chastened silence of storytellers with nothing to say. What is left is the disheartening gabble of the door-to-door salesman touting dead products: hair oil, nylons, fluorescent rotary phones, free tonsillectomies. Here are the editors of *Life,* unable to remove their feet from our doors, as they plunge into the next section of their special issue, which is entitled "2001–3000: The World as It Will Be."

We are about to enter a millennium of miracles. If a person cuts off his hand while fixing a lawn mower, doctors will be able to grow him a new one. Houses and cars will be made of materials that can fix themselves when damaged. There will be a white powdered food that is 90 percent protein and can be made to taste like almost anything.

And so on.

In the summer of 1976, Dad, I went to a Greg Stillson rally in Trimbull, which is in New Hampshire's third district. He was running for the first time then, you may recall. . . . I had one of my "flashes," only this one was no flash, Dad. It was a *vision,* either in the biblical sense or in something very near it. . . . I saw Greg Stillson as president of the United States. How far in the future I can't say, except that he had lost most of his hair. I would say fourteen years, or perhaps eighteen at the most. . . . If Stillson becomes president, he's going to worsen an international situation that is going to be pretty awful to begin with. If Stillson becomes president, he is going to end up precipitating a full-scale nuclear war. . . it's not going to be just two or three nations throwing warheads, but maybe as many as twenty-plus terrorist groups . . .

Like EliJah hiding in his cav

fish's belly, I thought I woul

Wait and see if the precondition

began to come into place. I woul

in the fall of last year the hea

r Jonah, who ended up in the

just wait and see, you know.

for such a horrible future

robably be waiting still, but

ches began to get worse.

Pretty exciting, huh?
But not, perhaps, really very *relevant*?

Everybody knows that the boat is leaking. Everybody knows the captain lied. Everybody got this broken feeling like their father or their dog just died. Everybody talking to their pockets. Everybody wants a box of chocolates and a long-stem rose. Everybody knows.

Everybody knows that the Plague is coming. Everybody knows that it's moving fast. Everybody knows that the naked man and woman—just a shining artifact of the past. Everybody knows the scene is dead, but there's going to be a metre on your bed that will disclose what everybody knows.

Everybody knows that you're in trouble. Everybody knows what you've been through, from the bloody cross on top of Calvary to the beach at Malibu. Everybody knows it's coming apart: take one last look at this Sacred Heart before it blows. And everybody knows.

—LEONARD COHEN, "EVERYBODY KNOWS"

What's missing, of course, is the frame of some sort of story. What kind of world will it have to be for all these miracles to work? And, in a world full of billions of human beings occupying less and less space, who'll benefit?

We all know that modern technology has been creating medical miracles for several decades now, but we also know that it's been getting harder and harder for anyone to know if their local hospitals, or health-care provider, will actually have on hand the particular spanking new hand you or I might need after fixing our lawn mower—which assumes we'll be one of the tiny elite remaining on planet Earth wealthy enough to afford (1) a lawn mower and (2) a lawn. It has been estimated that in the United States, perhaps uniquely, as much is spent yearly on lawn care as on educational books. But this use of affluence is not universal even in America; the health-care gap between what the rich can afford and what the poor can pay for is wider than it has ever been in human history, and every year the gap is widening.

You don't have to be a fanatical left-wing proponent of socialized medicine to wonder just how much you might have to *pay* to have doctors grow you a new hand. You might live in the wrong place. I might earn less than a hundred thousand a year.

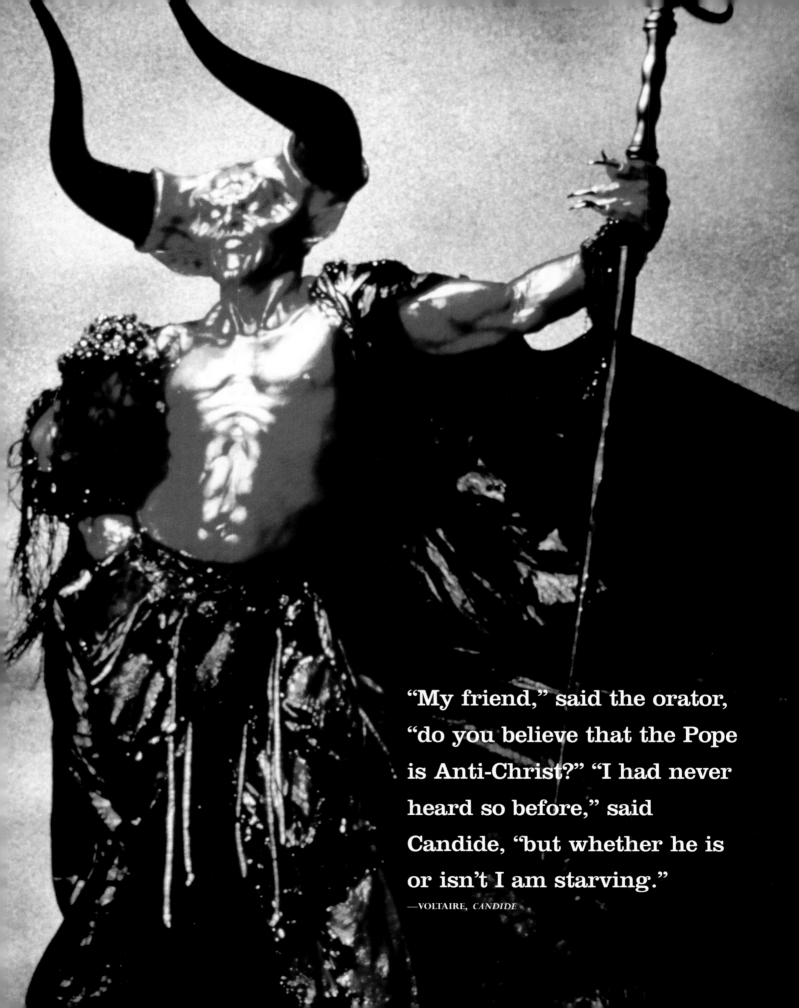

"My friend," said the orator, "do you believe that the Pope is Anti-Christ?" "I had never heard so before," said Candide, "but whether he is or isn't I am starving."
—VOLTAIRE, *CANDIDE*

We have reason to be afraid. This is a terrible place.

—JOHN BERRYMAN

So we are both *anxious*.
The future is an anxious place to look forward to.

We may never be able to find the thread that leads futureward.

We may die first, in this darkness at the end of history; and if we do find the future, we may not be able to afford it.

And when people who should know better, and who are paid to know better—such as the two dozen editors of *Life,* and their scores of experts—talk about the next thousand years as though there were nothing to be anxious about, as though (in effect) there were nothing really to talk about, then *they* make us anxious.

Well, the last thing I remember before I stripped and kneeled
Was that trainload of fools bogged down in a magnetic field.
A gypsy with a broken flag and a flashing ring
Said, "Son, this ain't a dream no more, it's the real thing."

—BOB DYLAN , "SEÑOR (TALES OF YANKEE POWER)"

They advertise the end times by the vacancy of the noise they make. They make us feel apocalyptic. They make us feel that profound anxious, claustrophobic panic that reoccurs historically whenever our "masters" are adrift.

The special issue of *Life* is no accident. The old ways of understanding our nature and destiny, as human beings on a small planet, have proved inadequate to the task. In our hearts, we no longer believe we know what is really happening to us or to our world. The special issue of *Life* is an infomercial for a dead product. We regret this. We regret this more deeply than we can say, because it was that dead product that made us what we are today. So we feel a horrible mixture of anxiety and nostalgia—as though the end times had entered our bones, like radiation. And we don't know what to do.

We sit at the edge of our seats, at the end of a century that gloried in change, and we find that the savants and politicians and advertising men and scientists who gloried in that change—and who were instrumental in persuading us all to keep our feet off the brakes—do not know what to make of the new worlds they have helped create.

But the possibility exists no matter how scary it may seem
That paradise was once the world and it wasn't a dream
The earth was our heaven and we didn't know there were rules for us to break
And maybe now we'll find out too late what a clever hell we can make
Whoops
Whoops

—J. POPPER, "WHOOPS"

Black & White, M.C. Escher

It is a bit like one of the famous reality-twisting drawings of M. C. Escher in which X changes into Y by small, seemingly simple stages that amount, in the end, to a final transformation beyond belief, beyond understanding. We are white birds in a black world who have become black birds in a world that is white, with no return ticket. As far as our fathers and mothers are concerned, we have become *impossible*.

But wait. We're being unfair. Nixon may have downsized the space program, may have demoralized the story of America, but no one could claim that he *wanted* to prepare the way for the Antichrist. The editors of *Life*, in a tone of unison cheer that marks their enterprise throughout, may have downsized the story of America, may have demoralized all of us who still read magazines, but no one could claim they *wanted* to end their epic of the rise of the West with a wet, plotless plop.

So it's only fair to let them try again. Here. Let the editors defend themselves against the imputation, which

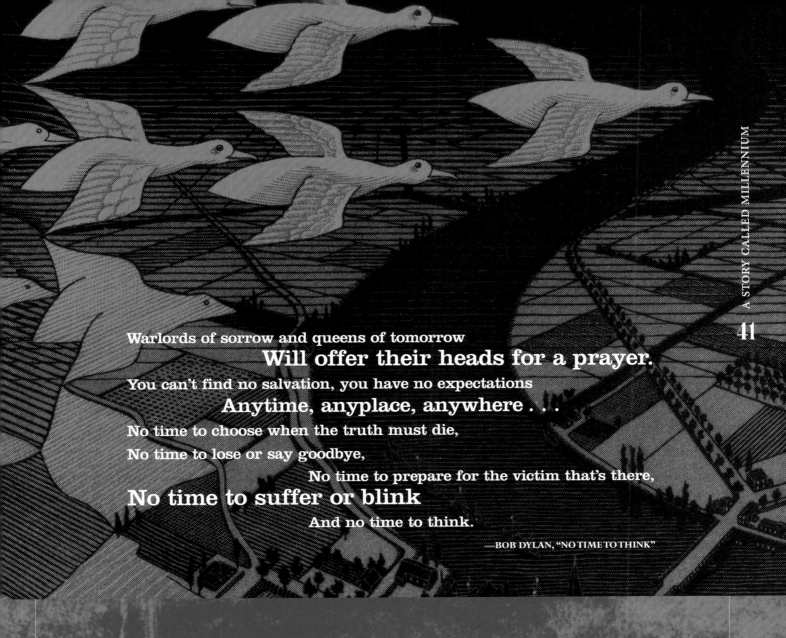

Warlords of sorrow and queens of tomorrow
Will offer their heads for a prayer.
You can't find no salvation, you have no expectations
Anytime, anyplace, anywhere . . .
No time to choose when the truth must die,
No time to lose or say goodbye,
No time to prepare for the victim that's there,
No time to suffer or blink
And no time to think.

—BOB DYLAN, "NO TIME TO THINK"

we have laid down, that they are agents of anomie, cultural despair, storylessness, dread, and anxiety, *avant couriers* of the end times.

So. Back to the future. The next thousand years, according to the editors of *Life,* may be something like this:

We do not know when, if ever, we will have robot slaves, orgasmatrons or time machines. But we do know that whatever miracles the next millennium holds, all will be wrought by the same genie: the computer.

So now we know. *There is nothing new here.* When the editors of *Life* look hence they see nothing but trailers for old "sci-fi" movies.

Beneath the smiley-face of this Futurama vision lies the Waste Land.

Between the lines of their cheerful paragraphs of prognosis, paragraphs that work on readers as a cumulative depressant, as an *abandonment,* we see that the editors of *Life* are of the opinion—though they express themselves only covertly—that human history has come to an end. It has been replaced. Their special issue is about not triumph but requiem. "Hold onto your hard drives," they conclude, not very relevantly, and perhaps unaware that hard drives are phallus-shaped, "it's going to be a hell of a ride."

What they don't say is who'll be steering. Not us.

What we're being told is that history will no longer be a human story. But the problem here is that human stories are the only kind of stories we know, and that we have been left alone, each of us, in the dark, to continue telling them. Our "masters" have abandoned the task; and it is surely the case that when computers evolve to the point they can tell stories, they will not be telling them to us. In the meantime, in the dark, we grab at straws, at Nostradamus, at end times. We remember the story of the Antichrist. *Anything goes.*

The real problem with theories of millenarianism is the narrowness of the concept itself. It is not quite the same thing as apocalyptic belief, which maintains that mankind is nearing the End of the World as we know it but does not necessarily imagine a violent or sudden change. All millenarianism is apocalyptic (from the Greek word meaning "to unveil"), but all apocalyptic belief is not millenarian: far from it. Classic millenarians, from self-flagellating medieval peasants to Sioux Ghost Dancers, are often people who, if not clinically mad, have reached what George Rosen has called "the wilder shores of sanity." They are relatively easy to distinguish from the population at large, and never more so than at the moment. We see this in the disturbing phenomenon of doomsday cults and sects, which is assuming greater prominence as we approach the end of the second Christian millennium. The world is still trying to make sense of the gas attack on the Tokyo underground by the unquestionably millenarian Aum Shinrikyo cult. The terrifying prospect of cult members releasing poison gas into the nerve centre of our cities reinforces our image of millenarians as outside, alien invaders. It reinforces the comforting and misleading impression that there is no common ground between fanatical millenarians and the rest of society.

—DAMIAN THOMPSON, *THE END OF TIME: FAITH AND FEAR IN THE SHADOW OF THE MILLENNIUM*

Anti-Christ will have been born upon Midsummer Night. And in a land, we might imagine, of nearly equal night and day. Of not much difference in the seasons, but with sudden thunder in the mountains. Lightning is like the stripes of light upon the tiger. It leaps out of the brakes; or, with no warning, into the great open fields of starlight. Where it couches, or lies panting. The tiger is his sign; not the cold clear stars of frosty nights. Not the New Year; but the middle, or autumn, of the old. . . .

He does not hide within the wall. He will not be caught coming out between the stones. He does not crawl out to lie in the sun. He has not had a winter of long sleep. Was he born, like King Pyrrhus, with the teeth already showing in his gums? It would be easy to know him, were there but signs upon his body. But he has come, at random, like the sudden lightning. No one has told in whose family he will be born. We might search, high and low, at all times and places, and not find him. Where the dog star whines; where the ilex glitters; where the flames cluck like so many cocks and hens; where the ewe's milk is blue as rain; where the mirror, in the locked room, turns upon the wall; where the babe, in the eighth month, has cried out inside its mother's womb? Such are lesser wonders, but pointing in one way.

—SACHEVERELL SITWELL, "THE BIRTH OF ANTI-CHRIST"

But of course human beings are not very good at being impossible. We need to believe in ourselves; we need to believe we make sense; we need stories to live by. The upwelling apocalyptic anxieties that characterize the end of the twentieth century are symptoms of our refusal to be impossible. They are storm warnings from the human psyche. They are hints of a port in the storm, fragments of a story that will make sense of things.

For those of us humans on this planet who are—like the editors of *Life*—the heirs of a thousand years of Western hegemony, and whose dreams are haunted by a religious tradition extending back another couple thousand years, it's most likely that the story we hear—the story we tell—will take on at least some of the lineaments of the strangely hypnotic, archaic story of the end as displayed to us in the Bible, and subsequently by millenarians everywhere in the West.

The moment had come,
      I swallowed my gum,
We knew there'd be blood on the sand pretty soon.
      The crowd held its breath,
Hoping that death
      Would brighten an otherwise dull afternoon.
—TOM LEHRER, "IN OLD MEXICO"

That's what the editors of *Life* feel, between the lines.
Why didn't they say so?

The sound of human beings volunteering to utter words they do not believe is the sound of the end of a culture.

President Nixon and the special issue of *Life* are far more prophetic than either the ex-president or the editors of that special issue could have dreamed.

What they tell us is that the West is done.
      That there is nothing human left to tell.

That it is better to be anesthetized than to think. It is a mercilessly grim message. It is what our masters tell us under their breaths, ignorant of the fact that we can smell their breath; it is what they say in the secret whispering midnight gossip of the end we hear in our dreams

"Then I had another dream, that I was sitting on a throne strapped to the top of a wheel, and the wheel turned over, and I was thrown into a pit of snakes."
"The wheel is come full circle: I am here."
"Are you a bad dream?" he asked. "If you are, do not torment me."
—T. H. WHITE, *THE BOOK OF MERLYN*

and know is true.

No wonder we feel a bit apocalyptic about the futures raining down upon us. No wonder, given nothing to break our fasts in the ruins, we make up stories about the end. Out of the shambles, out of the trillions of bytes of data that flow by our eyes every day, out of random inputs of history or speculative thought or crank prognosis or prayer or pious hope, we who live in end times, we who have become impossible, are making stories

"The world of human society," Vico wrote, "has certainly been made by men, and its principles are therefore to be found within the modifications of our own human mind." Religious myths, in this context, were not picturesque inventions or lying fables, as the humanists and the rationalists in turn maintained; nor were they confused memories of extraordinary men as the Euhemerists believed. They were concrete and systematic ways of expression and of understanding reality: neither devils nor poetic constructs, but "true histories of customs," "civil histories of the first peoples, who were poets," "the first science to be learnt."
—FERNANDO CERVANTES, *THE DEVIL IN THE NEW WORLD: THE IMPACT OF DIABOLISM IN NEW SPAIN*

around the campfire about the bogies of the end. We should take some pride in the accomplishment.

I have set as my goal
to get so strong
I could peel onions
all day long
and never shed one tear—

I want my skin to thicken
so if I am panic-stricken
when post-nuke day gets here
I won't even feel the fear
as I watch me and the world
    disappear.

—JANE WAGNER, *THE SEARCH FOR SIGNS OF INTELLIGENT LIFE IN THE UNIVERSE*

JAMES STEWART
JOHN WAYNE
DANS UNE PRODUCTION DE
JOHN FORD

l'Homme qui tua
Liberty Valance
"THE MAN WHO SHOT LIBERTY VALANCE."

VERA MILES · LEE MARVIN · EDMOND O'BRIEN · ANDY DEVINE · KEN
REGIE JOHN FORD · PROD. WILLIS GOLDBECK

DE MAN DIE LIBERTY VALANCE NE

This is the
the legend
print the le

—THE MAN WHO SHOT LIBERTY VALANCE

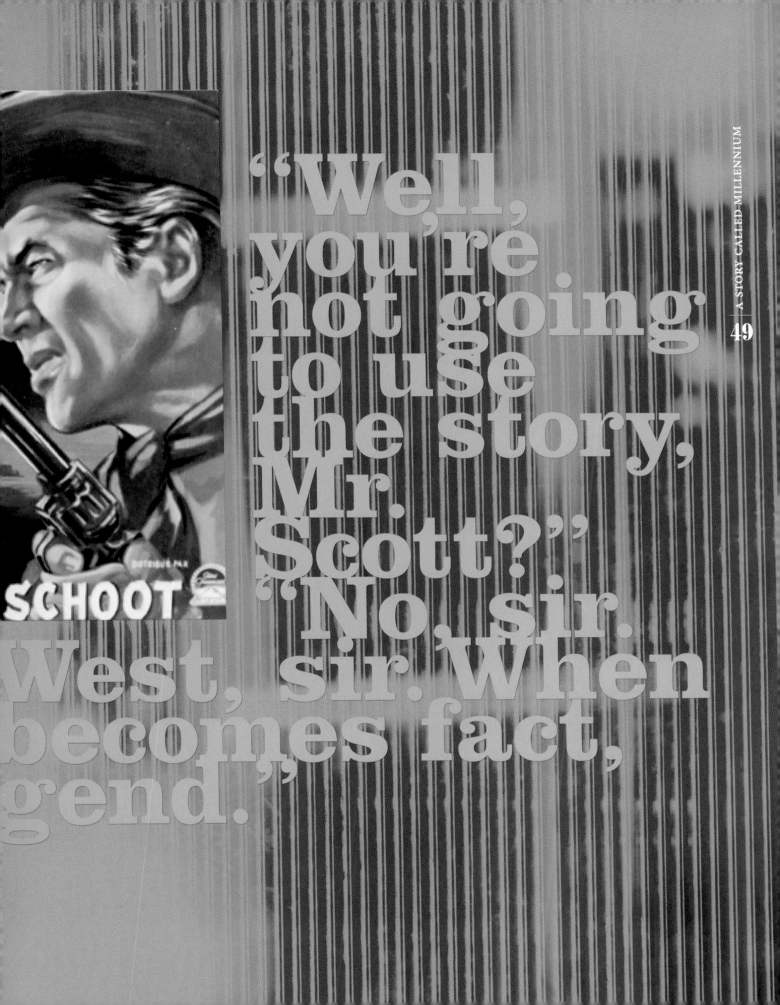

"Well, you're not going to use the story, Mr. Scott?" "No, sir.

West, sir. When becomes fact, gend."

The Garden of Earthly Delights (detail), Hieronymus Bosch

III

THERE IS NO SHARK

When we turn on the radio in a New York hotel room and hear Elvis singing "Heartbreak Hotel," we are seldom struck by the peculiarity of our situation: that a dead man sings.

In the context of the longer life of the species, it is something that only just changed a moment ago. It is something new, and I sometimes feel that, yes, everything has changed. (This perpetual toggling between nothing being new, under the sun, and everything having very recently changed, absolutely, is perhaps the central driving tension of my work.)

Our "now" has become at once more unforgivingly brief and unprecedently elastic.

—WILLIAM GIBSON

One of our deepest anxieties, of course, as the 1990s mount the asymptote to 2000, is that this story—which lurks within us—may turn out to be true. The end-of-time story we tell ourselves has been brewed out of varying ingredients: numerology, astrology, futurology, religious beliefs, ecological fears, the pressure of time, the growing claustrophobia of a species stuck to a planet too small to survive on, the end of the West, and an increasing spatter—like small knives to the heart—of what it seems appropriate to call toggle moments.

Definition

Toggle:

A switch between before and after. It is a moment in the world when a difference in degree turns visibly into a difference in kind. Visibility is the key. A toggle occurs when things not only change but *are seen to change*.

But let there be no mistake. The world we live in is far too complicated to understand—which is, of course, why so many patently inadequate explanations for the way things are jostle for lebensraum with more arduous (and partial) attempts to make sense of the course of history. We are in the middle of an era almost certainly unprecedented for the stupidity of the explanations most of its inhabitants claim to think make sense of things. Here's a stanza from the "prophecies" of Nostradamus:

The young heir to the British realm,
Whom his dying father will have recommended:
The latter dead: "Lonole" will dispute with him,
And from the son the realm demanded.

It is a quatrain that—if Lonole is meant to be London, and if London stands for Parliament, and if patrilineal succession is conveyed through the previous king's recommendation (rather than by inheritance), and if Prince Edward (who was forty-two in 1936) can properly be described as a "young heir," and if the year this all takes place *is* 1936—proves that Nostradamus *precisely* predicted the abdication of King Edward VIII. Which is nonsense, with the virtue of looking like nonsense to anyone but a numerologist. The problem with *Life,* whose special issue we were looking at, is that it does not look like nonsense.

But nonsense is our milk these days. From the shambolic (though rhetorically stunning) posturings of the Revelation of St. John the Divine to the latest Coca-Cola ad campaign seemingly designed to show American drinkers of American soft drinks how much the third world loves us, we are all mired—like waterbugs in oil slicks—in *nonsense*. It is no easy task to sort out the trivial from the significant.

We picked on the editors of *Life* for a while. But it is not only that crew of prognosticators who seem to be backing into the new century without a clue, who show us nothing but their own frightened faces as they totter backward over the cliff and down the long fall into tomorrow.

What's even worse than the sound of silence is having to listen to the jokers. The editors of *Life* may tell us, through their silence about now, that we have lost the story; but others—far more culpably—may tell us there's a story going down, all right, but that it's a joke.

Death is psychosomatic.

—CHARLES MANSON

A dinosaur joke, perhaps.

Almost at random, let us go back to a day like most other days at the end of the century, 15 February 1998, and take a look for a moment at a small human-interest news item that appeared that day, written in the usual human-interest style—cozy, condescending, designed to reassure us that we needn't lose sleep over whatever was being said. The news item appeared in the United Kingdom, in the pages of a "quality" weekly paper called the *Observer*, which is published each Sunday. As it is not bound to the wheel of a daily schedule, the *Observer* tends to concentrate on magazine-like think pieces. It claims to reflect on the implications of events. So if the editors of the *Observer* present a story about "rearranging the planet" in a jocular key, then they have *decided* that a jocular key is appropriate.

The news item of 15 February 1998 is a toggle story—though of course that term is not used. It's about yet another significant pause-to-think moment in humanity's inexorable "progress." "Without noticing it," the story begins, "humans have just passed yet another milestone on evolution's rocky road."

(We'll let pass the Whig language underlying this opening sentence, the shyly unarticulated presumption that evolution is a kind of progress, a set of milestones for humanity to hurdle en route to something higher. We have other fish to fry.)

Over everything else, we find a kicker line—a line of large type, halfway between a headline and a blur; it spreads across the eight columns (a full page in England) required by the story and the illustration, and it reads:
THE EARTH MOVES FOR ALL OF US AS JCB MAN SHIFTS MORE ROCK, SAND AND GRAVEL THAN ALL THE RIVERS PUT TOGETHER

Below this kicker, in larger letters, the headline itself reads:

HOLD ON, WILMA. I'M JUST

Occupying as much space as the actual text is a large cartoon showing characters made famous by the Hanna-Barbera *Flintstones* TV series. It is a drawing of Fred Flintstone and his dinosaur friend

So if the question here is "what is to be done" with the dinosaur, I do not have an answer, except "keep an eye on it." That is, pay attention to what is happening to it, try to make sense of it. The creature has an uncanny capacity for working both

REARRANGING
THE PLANET.

symptomatically and diagnostically. It expresses the political unconscious of each era of modern life, manifesting collective anxieties about disaster and extinction, epitomizing our own ambivalence toward our collective tradition. It always accompanies the disaster theme with a narrative of our own possible extinction, and how to avoid it.

—W. J. T. MITCHELL, *THE LAST DINOSAUR BOOK*

reposing comically in front of an office made out of rock. Below the cartoon, a caption reads: "Flintstone, alias *Homo erectus,* found a ready-made home and so had no earth to move."

The story itself begins, finally.

We learn that a day earlier, a geologist from Maine named Dr. Roger Hooke has given a talk to the American Association for the Advancement of Science. In this talk, Dr. Hooke draws some telling conclusions from the fact that modern Americans—whom he calls "*Homo bulldozerensis*"—are currently able to disrupt and shift from one place to another something like 7.5 billion tons of soil a year, mostly in the course of building houses, mining, and adding a few more miles to the fifty-foot-wide, two-million-mile-long strip of asphalt and concrete already given over to the cars they love so deeply. This is about thirty tons of rock, sand, and gravel a person, says Dr. Hooke, which is a lot of rock, sand, and gravel.

"By these crude calculations, the earth moved by humans exceeded that moved by rivers 25 years ago," he said. "With current rates of increase in our population and earthmoving capabilities, humans may be moving twice as much earth as all other geomorphic forces combined by the middle of the twenty-first century." Since no one can predict the long-term effect of this on the environment, the prospect, says Dr. Hooke, is "ominous."

As far as the *Observer* story lets us know, Dr. Hooke's presentation of these speculations, before a group of high-minded fellow professionals, is perfectly straightforward; he makes a clear and solid case that his speculative statistics should be treated with due seriousness.

We do know, after all, that there are billions more of us than there were a century ago; and we know that hundreds of millions of us, those who live in the Western world, have enjoyed an exponential increase in individual power—power, through the advances of technology, to do harm (and good). And we also know that the living surface of the planet we inhabit is fragile, that human beings in the twentieth century have been pretty hard on that living surface, and that the living surface we occupy in our relentlessly increasing numbers is not growing any larger. Most of us know—or should know—that we are getting very close to a point where we have exhausted all the exploitable virgin land the planet has left to offer.

So when we shift billions of tons a year of that precious living stuff about, without knowing the consequences of doing so (and Dr. Hooke makes it very clear we do not), then we are playing dice with a precious and diminishing resource. We are ripping away at the web of life, as though it were an infinite resource. As though the breast

The breast is shut.

—*THE LITTLE BOOK OF APHORISMS OF THE END*

of the earth will never dry. Simply to mention any of this—one might think—is necessarily to take it seriously. Because it is not a joke.

To make a joke about Dr. Hooke, who is talking about the world, is to make a claim about the kind of story that is appropriate to the world. It is to claim that the way of understanding the world that Dr. Hooke's findings represent, if taken straight, constitutes a wrong way of understanding the world. That Dr. Hooke is telling the wrong story. It means that his findings cannot be presented directly; they must be *displaced,* told within a frame of comic irony.

But this isn't all. Here again is the caption that "explains" the cartoon that "illustrates" Dr. Hooke's thesis: "Flintstone, alias *Homo erectus,* found a ready-made home and so had no earth to move." This rhetoric of comic irony may shape the *Observer* news item, but its claim—that *Homo erectus* (alias Flintstone) does not disturb the planet—is placed directly above this passage from the news item itself:

Homo erectus was building houses out of saplings and moving boulders for walls and floors about 400,000 years ago.

So. Not only does the Flintstone cartoon trivialize the story, making it visually clear to the readers of the *Observer* that the news item it accompanies is a kind of joke, it is also, in the context of the story itself, a lie.

This seems peculiar: that a story whose only real interest lies in its arguments is presented in a fashion that muffles, misrepresents, cross-dresses those arguments; that the point of the story has to be pried out of its context.

It is as though the real story were too hot to touch.

Or: The sleep of anxiety

"The whole universe is balanced between pairs of opposites—good and evil, night and day, up and down, winter and summer. And, on the whole, the state of equilibrium is maintained. But every now and then one side weighs heavier than the other. Things begin to tilt. More often in the direction of *down,* of darkness. Chaos encroaches. It is what we call the Sleep of Reason; society begins to crumble—"

"Wait, sir, wait! Stop! What's the Sleep of Reason?"

"It is what happens when the level of wickedness in several people's minds begins to combine together and forms a force that can, temporarily at least, overcome the forces of honor and good sense and law. What—for instance—caused the hole in the ozone layer? It was greed and stupidity, a rush to make profits before the dangers of new industrial processes had been thoroughly explored. So, what resulted? Monsters found their way in."

"But—but,—but someone *sent* the monsters—who did that? Why?"

"It was the total sum of all that greed and wickedness in people's minds. We give it a name. We call it Satan, the Prince of Dark. Human beings who surrender totally to this force may become temporarily endowed with *super*human attributes."

—JOAN AIKEN, *THE COCKATRICE BOYS*

breeds monsters.

The most profoundly interesting and distressing aspect of this story is precisely the anxiety

And I lift my glass to the Awful Truth
which you can't reveal to the Ears of Youth
except to say it isn't worth a dime
And the whole damn place goes crazy twice
and it's once for the Devil and once for Christ
but the Boss don't like these dizzy heights—
we're busted in the blinding lights
of closing time

—LEONARD COHEN, "CLOSING TIME"

it clearly generated in the minds of those presenting it.

If Dr. Hooke is a nut (clearly he is not, although no doubt there is room for *scientific* debate over the validity of his methodology and results), then there was no point in publishing the story at all. If it's not true or arguable, then it's neither funny nor revealing about anything.

If, on the other hand, Dr. Hooke is a reasonable man saying something reasonable, then the only reason for the *Observer*'s treatment of that story must relate to the psychological state of those who generate that newspaper, or a sense that their readers, in this instance, needed to have a potentially frightening truth told so that it was in effect *untold*. Not only did professional journalists (truth seekers of our culture) trivialize a story whose only point was a serious one, they demonstrated in addition a malaise so deep—a conversion hysteria so domineering—that it warped savagely their capacity to present the news. By framing

Look sometimes on the darker side of things.
—SUNDIAL MOTTO

the story (pun intended) in a manner designed to contradict it, they transform a report concerning the nature of what might be happening to this planet, as the end times near, into a surreptitious but blatant joke.

When one thinks of conversion hysteria, one thinks of Steven Spielberg's *Jaws,* of the scene in which the mayor of the resort refuses to close the shark-threatened beach.

"There *is* no shark," said the mayor hopefully.

Most of us remember what happens next.

Or it makes us think of "sci-fi," makes us think of the kind of story the *Observer* editors tried to transform a dangerous thought into. "Sci-fi," or retro sf, could be called a conversion hysteria of genuine sf, whose authors attempt to face into the wind of tomorrow. "Sci-fi" is *Star Wars,* which arrived on the scene in 1977 when "America was tired of complications," as Eric Harrison argued recently in the *Los Angeles Times*:

Vietnam, Watergate and social unrest had rattled our brains. The oil embargo showed us how weak we had become. We'd lost our sense of who we were. George Lucas reminded us. Two years later we elected Ronald Reagan president and it was Morning in America again.

What *Star Wars* did for America in 1977, *The Phantom Menace* threatens to do for America in 1999. It threatens to help Americans, not for the first time, reduce their anxiety levels by treating the world as deniable. This makes *The Phantom Menace*—and those adults who get a warm feeling from watching it—very frightening.

There. **is no** shark.

Slowly the poison the whole blood stream fills.

It is not the effort nor the failure tires.

The waste remains, the waste remains and kills.

It is not your system or clear sight that mills

Down small to the consequence a life requires;

Slowly the poison the whole blood stream fills. . . .

Not to have fire is to be a skin that shrills.

The complete fire is death. From partial fires

The waste remains, the waste remains and kills.

It is the poems you have lost, the ills

From missing dates, at which the heart expires.

Slowly the poison the whole blood stream fills.

The waste remains, the waste remains and kills.

—WILLIAM EMPSON, "MISSING DATES"

We know the editors of the *Observer* are not as stupid as they're making themselves sound. When they lie to themselves, and to us, we can sense it. There is a fog of wrongness in the air. Like children told lies, we choke on it.

Our leaders are trying to tell us bedtime stories, but they have lost the knack.

To build, brother, one has to build, to plane—to plane the House of God: and likewise: here are both furniture and woman, and all the rest. The resurrection of the dead, brother, will take first place in the memory, in the spirit: the dead will come to pass their time with us, friend; that's the way it is. . . ."

Quietly his face crawled out of the homespun coat, and now it looked quite different: white and luminous: neither pale nor flushed—the carpenter had become all white. The sleet whipped them more and more; the smoky wisps of cloud rushed fussily from horizon to horizon; there was no end or beginning to their armies.

—ANDREY BIELY, THE SILVER DOVE

God Creating the Universe, William Blake

WHAT TO DO IN DREAMLAND

Part Two
till we're dead

We're a species that does not like being alone. We gab all the time, because when we are not gabbing, or thinking about gabbing, we die a little inside. We are a gregarious species. We share our joys and fears. We do not breed alone. The only sex that counts is with other people. We come together in groups around the campfire and sing songs about love and the army and the fall of night. There is always somebody with a better voice than the rest of us, and bigger lungs; you can always hear that voice, leading the song. It is usually the voice of a man, but not always. It is the voice of the leader of the pack, the emperor of the round world. There is always an emperor around.

Maybe we've grown up enough, as a species, to understand that constitutional emperors are a good deal more palatable than absolute emperors. But we still need them. We elected President Clinton. We elected Tony Blair. We even elected Boris Yeltsin. But where are they now that we need them? Now that we need a story . . .

What we hear, instead, is the noise of nothing—the dead deafening noise of nullity that issues from the editors of *Life* and the writers for the *Observer*. The noise that our "leaders" make at the end of time is the deafening silence of bankruptcy, and what we have to look forward to is almost certainly more of the same. When our leaders declare bankruptcy, they impoverish us all.

It is no wonder, perhaps, that so many of us fund our lives with anything but the future, with retro obsessions and conversion hysterias and dreams of alien abduction (dreams that absolve us of any concern for the future at all, because the future has been taken out of our hands by others).

In 1999 we are spelunkers in an icy cave, with no direction except the direction of slide, and we'll try anything to get a foothold, to make time stop, to turn it back, sideways, away.

Anytime but now. Anywhere but next.
Here are some of the things we do in Dreamland till we're dead.

THE TAMAGOTCHI GESTURE

Wednesday, 8 April 1998, 1:01 P.M. EDT

FRENCH DRIVER SAVES VIRTUAL TAMAGOTCHI PET, KILLS CYCLIST

MARSEILLE, FRANCE (REUTERS)—A FRENCH DRIVER KILLED A CYCLIST AND INJURED ANOTHER AFTER SHE TOOK HER EYE OFF THE ROAD TRYING TO SAVE HER TAMAGOTCHI VIRTUAL PET, POLICE SAID WEDNESDAY.

THE 27-YEAR-OLD WOMAN BECAME DISTRACTED WHEN THE ELECTRONIC PET, WHICH WAS ATTACHED TO HER CAR KEY RING, STARTED TO SEND OUT DISTRESS SIGNALS. SHE ASKED A COMPANION IN HER CAR TO ATTEND TO THE TAMAGOTCHI BUT IN THE CONFUSION SHE FAILED TO NOTICE A GROUP OF CYCLISTS ON THE ROAD AHEAD AND SLAMMED INTO THE BACK OF THEM. ONE DIED INSTANTLY AND ANOTHER WAS TAKEN TO HOSPITAL.

POLICE SAID THE WOMAN WAS ARRESTED AFTER SUNDAY'S ACCIDENT NEAR THE SOUTHERN CITY OF MARSEILLE. A MAGISTRATE WAS INVESTIGATING WHETHER CHARGES SHOULD BE BROUGHT.

The Tamagotchi is an interactive toy that was invented in Japan a few years ago and soon became extremely popular worldwide. It was not cheap at first, but in 1999 cheap models are available. Tamagotchis can now be found everywhere, not only in the households of the lucky. Children were the first to love them, and feeding-frenzy scenes were common a few years ago at those toy stores lucky enough to wangle stock; there is some evidence, however, that children got bored with Tamagotchis rather more quickly than their parents, who find the demandingness of the device strangely seductive. Certainly the hectic early days have passed.

But Tamagotchis are everywhere now.

The basic Tamagotchi toy (or device) is a plastic egg-shaped oval, small enough to couch in the palm of a child; in the center of the oval is an LCD display. Except for the display, Tamagotchis rather resemble the polished worry stones that folk traditionally carry about their persons and rub occasionally for luck or to remind themselves who they are today. But worry stones are mute. Inside the Tamagotchi toy, as we are meant to imagine, resides a small, far-from-mute smiley-face spirit, perhaps an infant or a genie.

Worry stones are typically owned by people who have lapsed from, or who never belonged to, the Roman Catholic Church; for these people, they work as a kind of secular substitute for a rosary or prayer beads. There is a difference, of course. Prayer beads proper are portals into a complex universe governed by human and divine interactions; in a sense that worshipers may deem holy, prayer beads are profoundly not mute. Worry stones, on the other hand, have always been thought of as secular: They mean nothing more than what we import into them, on our own. That is, in the West they are not normally thought of as having magical properties. But they are soothing. **To stroke a worry stone is to practice doing something meaningful.**

The Tamagotchi toy is, in other words, closer in function to the prayer bead than it is to the worry stone. It is the prayer bead come to "life." Although they do not evoke for us the kind of meaning system that prayer beads generate for worshipers within the Catholic Church, Tamagotchi toys do make us act as though we had received a message—nay, a commandment—from beyond.

Tamagotchi toys may be small, but they are about as easy to ignore as a dominatrix on a roll. Within the rectangular LCD readout, articulated through beeps and a variety of graphic enhancements, lies the neotonous image of some sort of infant, generally human in the earlier models, but of any number of species—real or imaginary—in more recent models. (It is in reality, of course, a readout generated by a computer chip.) This needy infant creature stares beguilingly out through the LCD window as it makes its demands.

Beneath the LCD readout the child (or, increasingly, the adult) will find several buttons, usually three. At the Tamagotchi toy's command—that is, whenever a particular distress signal is emitted by the infant within the toy, via a series of highly audible beeps; this call may come at any hour of the day or night—these buttons need to be pushed in one of a very large number of combinations. According to the combinations pressed, the ghost in the machine will thrive or not thrive, defecate or become constipated, sicken or wax healthy or die.

Tamagotchi teaches children—who will soon be adults in the twenty-first century, if we pass the gates into tomorrow—to respond with "caring" gestures to a message generated at random but according to arbitrary fixed rules, and without any actual needs being represented over and above the computer chip's "need" to have its message responded to. Children, in other words, are taught to perform caring interactions *on command,* as the essentially passive participants in a game controlled from elsewhere.

Tamagotchi imports extrinsic and coercive commands into intimate parts of the human world where, once upon a time, meaning was "naturally" generated. The focus has shifted from within the child, where meaning previously was presumed to reside, to the obedience of the child to a meaning-generating electronic environment.

It is the sort of toy that teaches children where the action is. As the news item quoted above shows, the Tamagotchi toy's demands for attention—always with the threat that if those demands are not attended to *immediately*, the toy may well die—extract a fixated, tunnel-vision response from the human being who is "playing" its game.

The Tamagotchi toy, being very much clearer than life, turns its players away from life.

So, even though the toy itself may turn out to have been a fad, the implications of the device are quite extraordinarily wide-reaching.

That turning away from life in order to marry gear whose main function is to parody life at a profit for others may be called the Tamagotchi gesture.

Going further afield, it might be worthwhile to refer to the fact that much of today's culture style bewilderingly (to some) treats the future as a solarized mirror image of the past, as though the end of the century were some unimaginably vast buffer we were running up against. Today's culture style, by pushing over the rim of the edgy, gives us a chance to play out that overwhelming sense of meaningless drift so many of us feel as we are washed down the long chute toward the year 2000, where we may find that the cocoon we have woven is indeed a terminus.

Some years later, I met Maurice Grimaud, then retired, and asked him what he felt during the May Events [the strikes and demonstrations in France, May 1968]. "A kind of joy," he said. "I was interested in living through events which, at every moment, I had a feeling were important. Government had broken down. I found the experience invigorating, a tonic."
—PETER LENNON, "A KIND OF JOY"

The irony is that, while conspicuously claiming to gift us with the ability to fulfill ourselves, the culture style of the 1990s actually works in an entirely different fashion. The culture of 1999 is the culture of the Tamagotchi gesture.

Here is some copy from a 1998 ad published in *The New York Times Magazine* on behalf of Breitling, a firm specializing in the manufacture and sale of retro mechanical watches:

Favored by pilots and aircrews since 1952, the Old Navitimer's mechanical chronograph displays the classic good looks of a 1950s-style timepiece, with slide rule built into a ruggedly water-resistant steel case. Early Navitimer models were a familiar sight in the cockpit of the Lockheed Constellation, whose four 2,250-hp motors provided this airliner with a range of more than 2,400 miles at a cruising altitude of over 16,000 feet. Providing a power reserve of at least 42 hours, the Old Navitimer self-winding chronograph measures times from 1/5th second to 12 hours plus intermediate and cumulative flying times when needed.

This advertising copy is very rich.

It invokes a world that has long disappeared—the world of mechanical watches themselves, a world that featured the awful Lockheed Constellation (I remember bouncing around inside their claustrophobic cabins, at the seeming mercy of every tiny storm from Chicago to St. Louis, in the early 1950s; and I don't want to go back there, not *really*). This appalling plane was a flagship for Trans World Airlines, itself a dodo long run over by faster firms, and it is in this world of bad planes and faltering airlines that we are meant to imagine ourselves *capable of operating a slide rule.* (Does anybody know anybody who can even *remember* how to operate one?) It is a world of illuminated dials and polished metal and corporate logos that were eternal; it was a world you could touch.

But you can't touch it now.
Not really.
When it was real, it was real.
In the hands of Breitling in 1998, it is Tamagotchi.
You do not touch Tamagotchi. Tamagotchi touches *you*.

A Tamagotchi watch may be defined as a watch that must be wound; if you do not wind it, it dies. The fabled inaccuracy of the mechanical watch—an inaccuracy that is totally obsolete in a world of digital timekeeping—is an inherent aspect of the Tamagotchi watch. Constantly inaccurate, and constantly in need of caring supervision to be of any earthly use at all, a Tamagotchi watch exists in 1999 solely in order to be inaccurate, and to need care, usually from a man of means. It is another way of defining the Tamagotchi gesture: the circular movement of a human arm winding a "self-winding" mechanical watch—which is, of course, anything *but* self-winding, and which cannot keep time—so that it will not "die."

Everywhere in the world today we see people so desperate for meaning in their lives that they will wind watches.
—THE LITTLE BOOK OF APHORISMS OF THE END

A play by Kara Miller called *Tamagotchi Heaven* was recently produced in Edinburgh. After a brief, unsatisfactory fling in the real world, with a real (though pretty awful) lover, the young protagonist of the play becomes obsessed with her Tamagotchi. At the "climax" of the play, she bares her breasts and masturbates with the thing. The play becomes silly afterward—the Tamagotchi turns into an offensively cuddly human dancer who talks baby talk at the protagonist—but at its deeply melancholy heart it is pure Tamagotchi gesture.

It is the gesture of a people turning away from time.
It is the gesture of a people at the end of time.

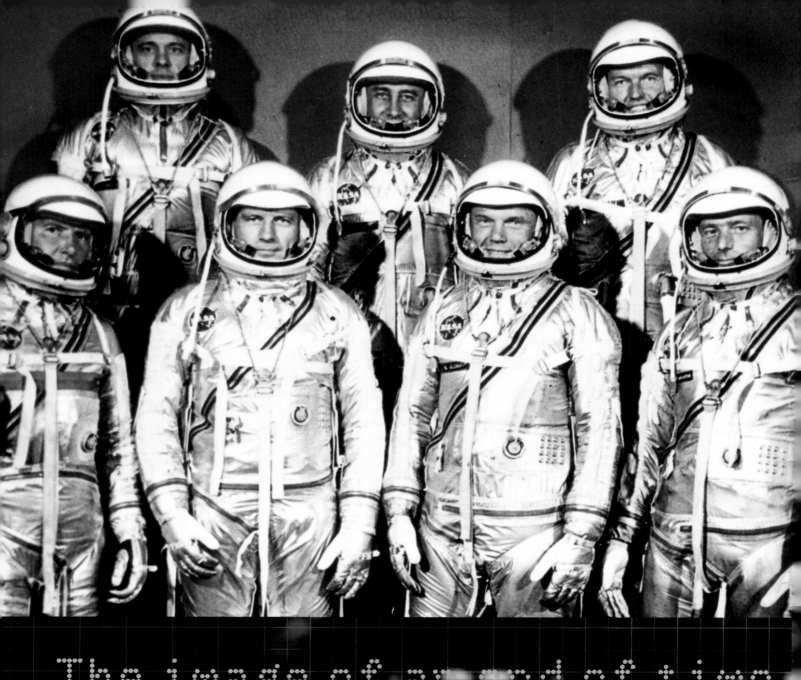

The image of an end of time

God as the ender of time beir

very powerful one. It has t

erwise it can drive peop

f the traditional role of

usurped by humanity, is a

e handled with care oth-

e over the edge.

As soon as we identify the Tamagotchi gesture—an elaborate, insectlike, compulsive action in response to a command generated solely to elicit that action—we begin to see it everywhere.

And we should be testing ourselves for it, just as we test ourselves for any of the opportunistic late-twentieth-century chronic ailments that—by mimicking the pandemics and contaminations of earlier centuries, and by eliciting a cavernous need on our own part to *have* them—ravage us incessantly. We should be testing ourselves for blight, just as Thomas Covenant, in *The Chronicles of Thomas Covenant the Unbeliever* (1977), by Steven R. Donaldson, tests his extremities for further incursions of leprosy.

The sign that you have found the Tamagotchi gesture at the extremities of your psyche is a false sense of well-being there—a lack of pain there that mimics well-being, but in fact reveals a numbness unto death.

Other phenomena that mimic or manifest the Tamagotchi gesture include:

1. Manned space flight as it exists in 1999.
2. Turning off Windows 98.
3. The craze for vinyl records. Writes Tom Cox: "In the grip of rabid millennium retrospection, where the twentieth century's icons are endlessly revived and re-evaluated, vinyl's popularity is on the increase—perhaps because of its retro kitsch value, perhaps because we never abandoned it on our own terms in the first place."
4. Astrology software.
5. A sustained sense of personal bereavement over the death of Princess Di.
6. VCRs.
7. Frequent-flyer programs—all of them designed to induce customers to purchase only those grades of tickets that are eligible to gain frequent-flyer miles. These tickets, often not the cheapest or most convenient available, engage the flyer in enormously complex interactive behaviors with the byzantine intricacies of a system designed (almost solely) to occupy the user. Frequent-flyer programs introduce a spurious sense of proactive meaning into the bizarre, Dantesque surrealism of modern flying in all its aspects.
8. Doc Martens.
9. Interactive exercise bicycles.
10. The World Wide Web—the enormous complicatedness of which has many explanations, technological, psychological, ideological, pathological. One of the more revealing explanations must be the suggestion that the complexity of the Internet is, half consciously, maintained in order to give its users an interactive function. A news story in *The New York Times,* 30 August 1998, reports that a study has found that frequent Internet

users almost invariably experience increased stress and depression—a finding that the study's compilers, funded by computer firms, found (amusingly) to be "counterintuitive."

11.   The new Volkswagen Beetle, designed to resemble the original Beetle, which has been around for more than sixty years (that is, for most of the twentieth century), and which was designed in the 1930s, when it was *functional* for the Beetle to look like a beetle, in order to perform with unprecedented cheapness and efficiency. But what might have been function in 1935 is Tamagotchi in 1999. Specific Tamagotchi features include a vestigial running board, which it would be dangerous to attempt actually to use, though it must be cleaned, stepped over, "obeyed" in a fashion completely without function; a reed inside the exhaust pipe whose only function is to make the new water-cooled engine sound something like the original air-cooled VW engine; an interior that replicates as far as possible the original egg shape but which, in order to meet the safety standards of 1999, features a vast dashboard that is dead space and has to be looked over, though there is a 1960s countercultural flower vase in the dashboard (which needs to have flowers put in it all the time, or it dies); and, because the front seat is now farther back (for safety), a tiny rear seat. In the end, the new Beetle is intensively recomplicated camp.

12.   Calendar packs containing pills in plastic bubbles that must be individually punched to release each pill.

13.   Any electronic/human interface whose immediate (if not consciously intended) consequence is to complexify the processes of interaction. The sign of this complexification is a communications process that requires elaborate obedience rituals (usually by the human being required to press keys) before the applicant is allowed to interact at all. An obvious example is voice mail.

14.   Modern computer games, which are radically different than their primitive predecessors such as Pong (an electronic tennis game) or Space Invaders. The skills involved in mastering these early games were akin to the motor skill of tying one's own shoelaces (once a child learns, painfully, how to tie shoelaces, it is as though it had never been a problem). But the modern games are different. Complex, involving, simulated 3-D arenas such as Doom and Quake require hugely complex interaction from their human players, a constant obedience to rules. This is in contrast to real-world games (or, dare we say it, life), where the actual ranges of possible action may not be more complex at any one moment than Doom's, but whose *potential* ranges of action are so infinitely variable that one needs to develop general strategies to "play" them, just as one needs general strategies to drive a car—in profound contradistinction to the motor skills required to shift gears. Modern computer games are elaborate conditioning machines that instruct players to follow extremely precise tactics that are of absolutely no use outside the game scenario. They distract users from the cold wind of reality, where general strategies are required to stay alive. They keep users in a universe of Tamagotchi gestures, where "action" is defined as pushing a button on command. A universe where "action" is *response*.

15.   The repentance of President Clinton.

16.   **Planet Hollywood.** The ostensible reason for going to a restaurant—ultimately to eat food—is obscured at Planet Hollywood by labyrinthine barriers and routines; the food itself, when it does at last appear, is significantly poor, an afterthought. The owners of Planet Hollywood knew (or thought they knew; the chain began to run into financial trouble around the end of the 1990s) that the food they sold was a pretext for displaced behavior on the part of their clientele, who paid to the protocols—the game rules that governed their access to the "goal"—the kind of attention owners of mechanical watches pay to winding them. Each Planet Hollywood "restaurant" is the inside of a Tamagotchi toy, blown up.

17.   Y2K.

18.   The *fin de millénium* itself.

19.   Us.

Definition

Decadence: A pain of glass, a pane in the ass.

We of the Western world have increasingly become actors of our own lifestyles. When we make faces in the mirror, we see through a glass darkly the gesture of the Tamagotchi.

Do you know what the great drama is? That I have put my genius into my life and my talent into my work.

—OSCAR WILDE, IN CONVERSATION WITH ANDRÉ GIDE

It is easier to obey instructions about who we are than to be who we are. Indeed, the whole of the twentieth century could eventually be understood as a series of Tamagotchi gestures for the use of the twenty-first century.

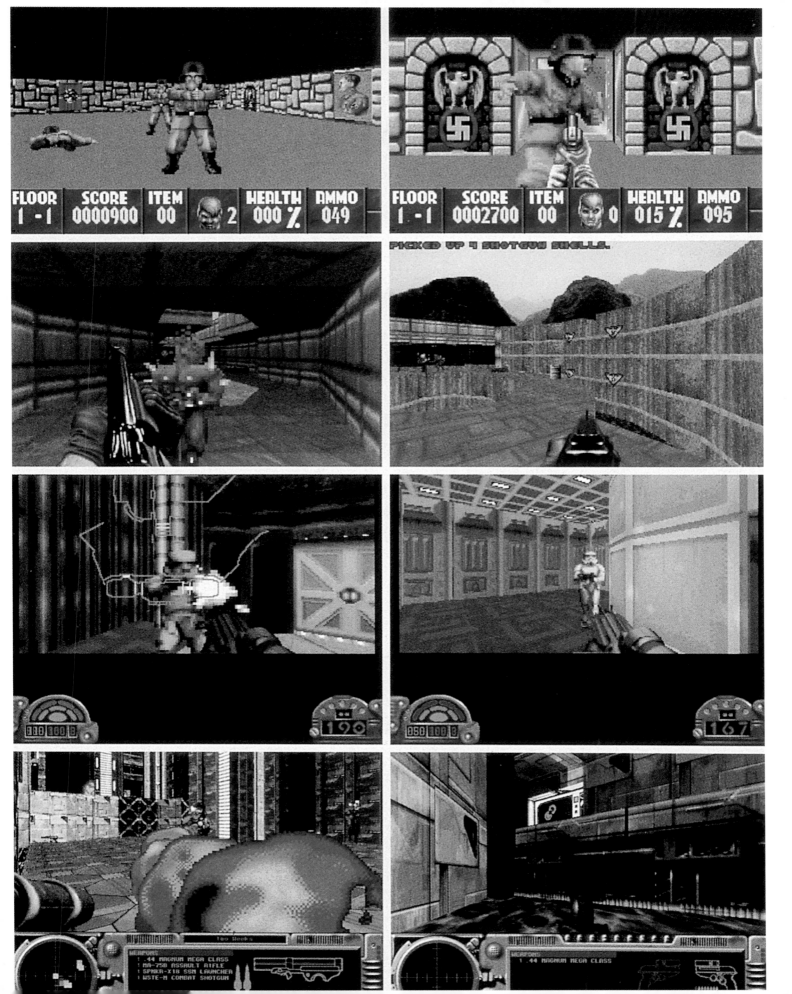

FLOOR 1-1 SCORE 0000900 ITEM 00 2 HEALTH 000 % AMMO 049

FLOOR 1-1 SCORE 0002700 ITEM 00 0 HEALTH 015 % AMMO 095

PICKED UP 4 SHOTGUN SHELLS.

Once upon a time there was a man who sought escape from the prattle of his neighbors and went to live alone in a hut he had found in the forest. At first he was content, but a bitter winter led him to cut down all the trees around his hut for firewood. The next summer he was hot and uncomfortable because his hut had no shade, and he complained bitterly of the harshness of the elements.

He made a little garden and kept some chickens, but rabbits were attracted by the food in the garden and ate much of it. The man went into the forest and trapped a fox, which he tamed and taught to catch rabbits. But the fox ate up the man's chickens as well. The man shot the fox and cursed the perfidy of the creatures of the wild.

The man always threw his refuse on the floor of his hut and soon it swarmed with vermin. He then built an ingenious system of hooks and pulleys so that everything in the hut could be suspended from the ceiling. But the strain was too much for the flimsy hut and it soon collapsed. The man grumbled about the inferior construction of the hut and built himself a new one.

One day he boasted to a relative in his old village about the peaceful beauty and plentiful game surrounding his forest home. The relative was impressed and reported back to his neighbors, who began to use the area for picnics and hunting excursions. The man was upset by this and cursed the intrusiveness of mankind. He began posting signs, setting traps, and shooting at those who came near his dwelling. In revenge groups of boys would come at night from time to time to frighten him and steal things. The man took to sleeping every night in a chair by the window with a loaded shotgun across his knees. One night he turned in his sleep and shot off his foot. The villagers were chastened and saddened by this misfortune and thereafter stayed away from his part of the forest. The man became lonely and cursed the unfriendliness and indifference of his former neighbors. And in all this the man saw no agency except what lay outside himself, for which reason, and because of his ingenu-

IT MUST BE SOMEBODY'S *FAULT* THAT I'M SICK

Hysteria is a profoundly hysterical term to use in order to describe hysteria. There are reasons for this. The term came into widespread popularity in the nineteenth century, in northern Europe, where the Industrial Revolution had transformed and destabilized whole civilizations virtually overnight; and where the sorcerer's apprentices who had triggered the modern nineteenth-century world were profoundly uneasy—though few of them admitted to any conscious dis-ease—about the nature of the rough beast they had unleashed. Being uneasy, and not being able to admit to the source of that unease, is how hysteria can start.

(We inherit that dis-ease. Only a few of us, however, have managed to inherit the obliviousness.)

Definition (expanded from the prologue)
Hysteria:

From *hysterion,* which is Greek for "womb." A disease where some scarring but inadmissible stress, which may be physical in origin but is usually psychic, surfaces as a symptom or symptoms seemingly unrelated to that original stress. Unlike the vague and shifting complaints of sufferers from hypochondria, these symptoms tend to be specific: paralysis; spasmodic tics; blindness; convulsions; sourceless infections with visible consequences such as rashes, fevers, fatigue. These psychosomatic symptoms *are not faked.* Hysteria is now commonly called by other names, including conversion disorder, dissociative identity disorder, and somatization disorder.

Another definition
Hysteria:

A cultural device that allows something that cannot be faced to be called something else.

To use the term *hysteria* under its first definition—certainly if you are an overworked, highly stressed, rigidly domineering nineteenth-century male on the thin ice of a precariously overswollen civilization—is to commit hysteria under its second definition. It is to mislocate a universal human symptom and complaint, to transfer it from the universal human space of the mind to the queerish innards of the female of the species. This is the pot calling the kettle black—which is yet another way to describe hysteria #2.

After all, if we in the twentieth century have learned one thing about ourselves as a species, it is that women—who work harder than men, who bear children and then raise them, who outlive men and stay healthier than men while they're doing it—are mentally much the tougher half of the human race, too. Unless they are corseted into unendurably restrictive social roles (as they have been, almost everywhere, until recently)—frustrating roles they dramatize through behavior and illnesses that illuminate their plight while seeming to have nothing to do with it—women are the realistic, pragmatic, flexible ones.

Men have traditionally spent their lives pretending to themselves and to the wife that business life is something mysterious and profound (something not to be understood by those outside the Law), but at the same time that it is something utterly natural and straightforward, that business is *real*. This is, of course, nonsense. Any grown woman (and any Martian who happened to be on an inspection tour) knows that business life is a hysterical conversion of childhood games (usually the kind you play with guns, or with bits of stuff one boy can bop another boy with). The difference between a playground bully and a junk-bond dealer lies in the superior self-knowledge of the playground bully.

Men are the hysterics of the race.

Hysteria might better be called *testesia*.
It is a plague of the late century.

During the great days of hysteria in the nineteenth century, when this affliction of urban stress was universally understood as a woman thing, it was not within the vocabulary of doctors and savants to understand as hysteria their responses to the revolutions so radically and so rapidly changing their lives.

But the paradigmatic Victorian gentleman—with his comical hard top hat, his elaborately stifling clothing, his lunatic self-esteem, his contempt for the working class, the female class, the class of colored folk outside the Law, the class of foreigners, the class of Jews, the class of Scotsmen, the class of vulgar Yankees—is a fount of hysteria.

It is impossible for this gentleman of the nineteenth century to see himself straight in the mirror, for if he did so, he would be able to see what had been avoided all his life: the anxious, fragile, all-too-human forked-stick *Homo sapiens* male, who is going to die. The playground bully, once he has "grown up," will do anything to avoid the mir-

A new extension of the human will to stretch their muscles with. It was the train.

CHICAGO NORTH WESTERN LINE

ror. He will build cities, ships, empires; he will invent weaponlike extensions of his limbs, tools of a range and power totally unprecedented in the previous history of the world; he will go to war; he will conquer the land, the nation, the continent, the world. He will do more than any other single category of human being to create the twentieth century.

It is now altogether possible—especially since he now has the tools to do the job—that he will succeed in converting his fear of mortality into the death of the planet.

For we are in the end times.

It is apocalypse now.

The world will not end because God has determined that our fate will be written in fire or ice, though fire and ice may dance attendance on the end; if the world ends, it will end because of hysteria.

We make the end of things.

> We are the beginning and the end of things.
>
>> If the world ends, it will end because we continue to refuse to see it.

Here is a minor example of hysteria at work. It may help give us some perspective in 1999 on the range of stresses we face—on the world we respond hysterically to.

Around about 1830, the industrialists and inventors who were making the modern world—starting with Great Britain—found a new tool to concentrate upon, a new extension of the human will to stretch their muscles with. It was the train. The introduction of the train was the greatest single blow that had ever been struck at the sense of reality of a nation.

Nowadays it is perhaps impossible to understand the impact of the railroad on the psyches of those who first experienced it. Before 1830, as Ralph Harrington of York University's Institute of Railway Studies notes in a 1998 *Guardian* article, most people had never experienced anything faster than running, but suddenly it all changed. The arrival of the railway "was symptomatic" (Harrington suggests) "of a society and culture suddenly speeding up, as ours is today. The railways marked a leap in speed which has never really been paralleled."

The difference between running and sitting in a carriage rocking through the air at eighty miles per hour (that speed was reached by 1854) is far greater than other physical difference a society has ever experienced. And the laying down of a jigsaw of rights-of-way across an entire country, a task that was accomplished with cartoon speed, more profoundly transformed that physical land than any previous single human intervention into the physical world.

Responses were various.

Charles Dickens blessed "the South Eastern Railway Company for realizing the Arabian Nights in the prose days." In other words, he saw the new network of travel as a network of story. He was both right and wrong.

Thomas Carlyle was convinced there was no way to stop a train once it had begun moving. He was more right than he could have known.

A shah from Persia, whose doctors were afraid he would suffocate at speed, seems to have ordered a private train, which he instructed not to exceed twenty miles per hour. He was probably suffocated by irate commuters.

Trains ate up the country, demolished whole sections of the cities. I live in London, a few hundred yards from the railway line that runs north from Euston Station, eventually reaching Glasgow. Dickens fluorescently described its construction in *Dombey and Son* (1848). A hundred and fifty years later, you can still see dozens of homes perched like flightless birds along the edge of the canyon through which the line runs. They sit at what was the heart of an urban crescent, which was torn apart by excavators who needed to moderate the gradient on the new right of way. A hundred and fifty years later, the scars are still visible—even though the railway network has, rightly, become thought of by social planners as a national treasure at risk of demolition, under the threat of that far more transformative intervention in the life of any nation, the automobile.

But this must be remembered: Everything inflicted by the train upon the England of 1850—just like everything the interstate system did to America after 1960 or so—was unconscious, unmeant, transformative, and irrevocable.

It was like a permanent change in the weather.

(The global warming to which thousands of smoke-burning locomotives contributed their mite may, in England, effect a genuine permanent apocalyptic change in the weather, for if the dynamic system that generates the Gulf Stream should weaken, because of a moderation in conditions in Arctic waters, the Gulf Stream itself could fade significantly, and Britain, sometime soon, could become as cold as Siberia. But progress—see below—is unstoppable.)

So trains are like the weather.

The Cities send to one another saying: "My sons are Mad
With wind of cruelty. Let us plait a scourge, O Sister City."
Children are nourish'd for the Slaughter; once the Child was fed
With Milk, but wherefore now are Children fed with blood?

The Horse is of more value than the Man. The Tiger fierce
Laughs at the Human form; the Lion mocks and thirsts for blood.
They cry, "O Spider, spread thy web! Enlarge thy bones, and, fill'd
With marrow, sinews and flesh, Exalt thyself, attain a voice.
"Call to the dark arm'd host; for all the sons of Men muster together

To desolate their cities!
Man shall be no more! Awake, O Hosts!"

—WILLIAM BLAKE, *VALA, OR THE FOUR ZOAS*

Which affects us down to the bone. But there is nothing that can be done about it. No wonder train travelers soon developed the hysterical set of symptoms that became known as "railway spine." Mr. Harrington:

It seems clear that most sufferers were really affected by nervous anxiety, but, then as now, there was a determination to find an organic, physical cause, rather than allowing the condition to be described as just "all in the mind." Doctors concentrated on the spine and the effect of jolting travel and speed on the delicate nerves in the spinal column.

Symptoms—we must never, of course, confuse them with the range of symptoms associated with chronic fatigue syndrome—included migraine, back pain, stiffness, personality disorders, insomnia, paralysis, and erotic stimulation of the libido through excessive rhythmical movement.

The victims were almost always men.

Let us contemplate a fact that we at the end of the twentieth century are only now getting used to. The engine of "progress" cannot be turned off, short of completely isolating the civilization in which it has taken root, which is impossible. Or bombing it back to the Stone Age, which is very unlikely to work. Progress—like an unstoppable plague, or the irreversible transformation of the protagonist of Stanley Kubrick's *2001: A Space Odyssey* (1968) into a child godling, or the vast gut-shaking crescendo of global warming—only has an on switch. That is a fact.

And the switch was turned to on before we were born.

Progress is change. Progress is unstoppable change.

It is like the weather.

Definition

Progress: A change that cannot unhappen.

The Victorian gentlemen who thought they were controlling the world were, as I've already said, sorcerer's apprentices. And somewhere deep inside they knew they were no longer in control of what they had unleashed. Deep inside they began to evince signs of the stress—the hysterical refusal to look upon their own faces in the mirror of their works—that has become a world-historical phenomenon.

Hysterically, they off-loaded the anxieties they were beginning to feel—the real and realistic anxieties attendant upon being caught in a world governed by the march of progress—and they gave these off-loaded anxieties the name of woman.

It's easy to be wrong when you're a bunch of guys in one club, traveling first-class.

On thin ice.

Ulcerated.

Death-bound.

Successful.

Mark Kingwell, author of the 1996 book *Dreams of Millennium,* has thought at some length about the relationship between a famous film, Fred McLeod Wilcox's *Forbidden Planet* (1966)—which is an sf version of Shakespeare's *The Tempest,* first performed three and a half centuries earlier—and our own world at century's end. What interests Kingwell is the transformation of Caliban from Shakespeare's monster (who has been understood as an image of the oppression of the native peoples of the world through Western colonialism) into an image of technology as a boundlessly dangerous manifestation of the unconscious self-destructive will or id of Prospero.

I quote Kingwell:

I keep coming back to its central conceit: the idea that technology gives us the power to facilitate our own inner violence, to make our dreams dangerously real. We have the power to destroy ourselves, this film suggests, only when our own unconscious wishes and fears are sent into the world. When, indeed, they *become* the world—a tissue of irrational fears, a screen onto which we project our various phobias and desires.

Prospero (both Shakespeare's and Walter Pidgeon's) can clearly be seen as engaged in hysterical displacement. At stake, of course, is the world.

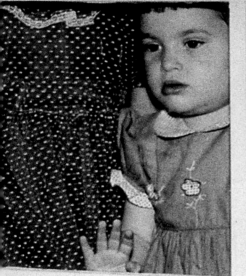

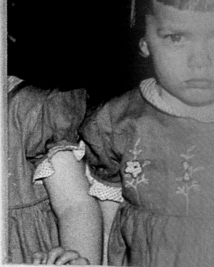

Order demands order.

—RODERICK SEIDENBERG,
POST-HISTORIC MAN: AN INQUIRY

Here is Elaine Showalter in her 1995 work *Hystories: Hysterical Epidemics and Modern Culture:*

In the 1990s, the United States has become the hot zone of psychogenic diseases, new and mutating forms of hysteria amplified by modern communications and fin de siècle anxiety. Contemporary hysterical patients blame external sources—a virus, sexual molestations, chemical warfare, satanic conspiracy, alien infiltration—for psychic problems. A century after Freud, many people still reject psychological explanations for symptoms; they believe psychosomatic disorders are illegitimate and search for physical evidence that firmly places cause and cure outside the self.

To Showalter's list one might also adduce the various "causation" panics that have proliferated in recent years. One might refer to the Chilean grape panic of 1989, when two grapes were found to contain a nonfatal amount of cyanide; in the Lady Macbeth purity purge that followed, two million crates of Chilean produce were impounded. Or the 1990 rumor that milk heated in microwaves caused brain damage in babies. Or the slightly later rumor that the chemical element daminozide in a brand-name spray called Alar, which was used on apples, caused cancer: After Alar was banned, it was duly discovered that mushrooms contain a thousand times as much daminozide as sprayed apples.

Or the mass withdrawal of children from vaccination programs in Britain in 1998, after researchers claimed to find—their findings have been described as "whimsical" by the British government—a correlation between measles and mumps vaccines and autism. The result? Thousands of children are now at risk from diseases once thought to have been eradicated. Or the sudden rash of symptoms reported in the United Kingdom later in 1998 by users of mobile phones, who claimed that they were being affected by radiation emanating from the headsets. Sufferers exhibited classic premillennial tension symptoms: ear burns, severe headaches, eye twitching, brain cancer, tumors. Some actually experienced what one might call stigmata, claiming that the actual image of the phone had been burned into their skin. In 1999 a firm called Microshield is manufacturing protective containers or shields, made of leather woven with nickel. Or, finally, the response of parents in the affluent West to an article in *Nature* that reported on a University of Pennsylvania medical school study that noted a correlation, but no causal link, between night-lights in children's rooms and shortsightedness. In Britain at least, thousands of parents began turning off night-lights, almost certainly diffusing trauma through the land as a result of this violent shift in the routines of infants.

"Hysteria," Showalter says, "is a mimetic disorder."

An Englishman, she says, might translate his sense of general helplessness

Because a cold rage seizes one at whiles
To show their bitter old and wrinkled truth
Stripped naked of all vesture that beguiles,
False dreams, false hopes, false masks and modes of youth;
Because it gives some sense of power and passion
In helpless impotence to try to fashion
Our woe in living words howe'er uncouth.

—DAVID THOMSON, *THE CITY OF DREADFUL NIGHT*

into a fatigue syndrome, but it is very unlikely that he would complain (as a native of Malaysia or south China might) that his penis is retracting into his body.

Hysteria also mimics the times.

The process can be complicated, because hysteria is not only a turning away from that which is the problem; it also constitutes an attempt to *specify* the problem. When the initiating problem—medical or psychological or cultural—is relatively simple, and when diagnosticians—whether medical or cultural—can make plausible connections between the original problem and the hysterical behavior that substitutes for it, then cures are possible. Hysteria can be a language that others understand. It can flag distress and attract succor.

But when the initiating problem is too big or convulsive to grasp, then the behavior that both turns away from and attempts to specify the malaise will itself tend to become convulsively extreme.

Caught—as Showalter says—in a time when "modern communications and fin de siècle anxiety" amplify and mutate the old hysterias, modern men and women of the Western world range far and wide in their attempts to pin the tail on the donkey; that is, to exhibit a range of symptoms that mimics—that lays the ghost of—an incomprehensible world.

Easier said than done.

The range of hysterias Showalter examines—similar to railway spine and mobile-telephone stigmata—amply demonstrates how hugely difficult it is to develop a hysterical symptomatology worthy of the task.

It also demonstrates the reality of that which may be caused, or partially caused, by an initiating conversion disorder. The suffering of those who experience medical symptoms is genuine. Chronic fatigue syndrome (CFS), for instance—which is known as myalgic encephalomyelitis (ME) in England, and which for a while was thought to be connected to the Epstein-Barr virus—has savagely affected the lives of thousands of intelligent, active, *proactive* men and women. The symptoms they feel—which include feverishness, aches, lassitude, swollen lymph glands, intolerable headaches, and

How come?
How come we're one
of the greatest nations
in the world . . .
and yet, there is this
feeling of
Doom? ## How come . . .

—RAY BRADBURY, "THE AFFLUENCE OF DESPAIR"

fatigue-related collapses after any form of exercise—may seem to occupy a gray region between hypochondria and good old-fashioned virus-caused killer flu. But most of these symptoms are measurable, and have been measured; and the symptomatology as a whole is consistent over large populations.

So it's a puzzle.

Either there is a single unknown organic cause that has not yet been discovered, despite years of intensive research, or something more complex—something, perhaps, that mimics something too vast and diffuse to be mimicked properly—lies at the root of CFS.

There is a clue in all the evidence. A high proportion of those who suffer CFS are professionals or those (like some women) whose complex daily activities require a similar intensity of effort in multiple-focus situations. CFS sufferers tend to be intelligent, overstressed, chronically dissatisfied with their accomplishments, bewilderingly busy without respite. To me personally (I do not have the disorder), people who suffer from CFS seem strangely *pulmonary:* When you meet one, you think of somebody who is holding his breath until there is time to breathe. CFS sufferers seem to live in the prayer that it will all add up in the end, that it *will* all add up to a coherent story, if only they don't stop first, fatally, to take a breather.

Their disease mimics an inability to breathe the world.

If CFS is a hysteria—and there is more medical evidence that significantly fails to support some simple, manly organic cause than you could shake a stick at—then it is a hysteria that assaults the men and women who are the officer class of late Western culture.

What CFS mimics is a culture that cannot make sense to its officer class.

I went to the cupboard, I opened the door,
I cried to my people, *O, it's not there!*
"How long did you think it would last?" said the cook,
Said the butler, "Does anyone care?"
But where is it, where is it? O it's not there,
Not there to be saved, not there to be saved,
If I'm saved it will not be there.

I ran to a plate, to a pig, to a dish,
An old china pig, a plate, to a pear,
Said, *To find it, O, I will look anywhere,*
Said, *Anywhere, Anywhere . . .* "Look anywhere,"
Said the plate as it laughed, "yes, look anywhere;
There's as good as here, there's as good as there—
For where shall you look to be saved?"

I said to my people, the plate, to the cupboard,
The pig on its platter, the pear, the pear:
O where is my salvation?
    "O it's not anywhere.
You break in my head like a dish," said the plate,
"A pig," said the pig, "a pear," said the pear—
Not there to be saved, go not there to be saved,
If you're saved it will not be there.

—RANDALL JARRELL, "SONG: NOT THERE"

Any life can be seen as a flow of information. Any life, therefore, is a kind of story. Those men and women whose job it is—in some fashion—to meditate upon that story (as writers and cartoonists and teachers do), or to operate significant joins in the grammar of that story (as doctors and lawyers and politicians do), endure lives that, when neither meditation nor grammar any longer makes sense of things, are peculiarly prone to disaster.

What CFS mimics is the loss of meditation or grammar from our world.

The natural inheritance of everyone who is capable of spiritual life is an unsubdued forest where the wolf howls and the obscene bird of night chatters.

—HENRY JAMES SR., *SUBSTANCE AND SHADOW*

Why howl ye so ye little Wolves?
Your Mammy's gone a hunting,
And if you're good she'll bring you home
Some bits of Baby Bunting.

—F. CARRUTHERS GOULD, *WILD NATURE*

I see your face, in every place, that I'll be going

I read your words, like black hungry birds, read every sowing

Spin and call, throw the ball, my name is Carnival

Sad music in the night, sings a stream of light, out of chorus

Voices you might hear, appear and disappear in the forest

Short and tall, come throw the ball, my name is Carnival

Stings of yellow tears, drip from black wired fears in the meadow

White halos spin, with an anger that is thin and turns to sorrow

King of all, hear my call, it's Carnival

Here there is no law, but the arcade's penny claw, hanging empty

The painted laughing smile, the turning of the stile, do not envy

Where the small can steal the ball, touch the face of Carnival

The fat woman frowns, at screaming frightened clowns that stand enchanted

And the shadow lion waits, outside your iron gates with one wish granted

Colors all, come throw the ball, my name is Carnival

Without a thought or sigh, you come to hypnotise the danger

In a world that comes apart, there is no single heart, and life is stranger

Wheel and call, cloud dreams all, in the name of Carnival

Yeah wheel and call, spin and call my name, oh it's Carnival.

—JACKSON C. FRANK, "CARNIVAL"

It does not mimic any kind of solution at all.

Most CFS sufferers are, in the end, too intricately involved in complex lives for them to be able to re-sort what they have learned about the world into the simplistics of millennialism.

It is an apocalyptic kind of disease.

Showalter examines several further syndromes of our time, all of which she strongly suggests are hysterical in origin. Some of her suggestions are undoubtedly controversial. After half a century of lying governments, it is very difficult for late-twentieth-century men and women, for instance, *not* to believe that Gulf War syndrome is purely and simply organic, nor are official attempts to dismiss the syndrome as "merely" psychological really very reassuring.

After all, a TV series such as *The X-Files* is structured around the assumption that "they" are lying to us,

Many of us would much rather that we could blame some other force or power for the things that we do. This, in fact, is the attraction of the dualistic and in particular the demonic vision of life. In a world of competing forces, in a world where Satan has power, what are we to do? Our worst actions can be ascribed, not to what we have done for reasons we have made, but to a force beyond us that has "power" over us. This desire to exonerate ourselves from the consequences of what we do, to find something or someone else whom we can blame for what in our actions and lives we do not like, is a very ancient desire. Today it still manifests itself.

—MARTIN PALMER, *DANCING TO ARMAGEDDON*

and that they never stop doing so. The main problem with *The X-Files*—though it is, after all, nothing but fiction—is that it is structured around the assumption that "they" are lying to us *for a reason*.

That they are hiding something.

Facts and figures. Corpses in a row. *Refrigerated rooms*. Plots and symmetries.
This is millennial thinking.

Good stuff for a story. It is more reassuring to think the government has evil plans afoot than to think it has no plan at all.

But when it enters the real world, it sickens the real world, whose workings are not best uncovered through a process of believing in least likely outcomes.

Printers finde by experience that one Murther is worth two Monsters, and at least three walking Spirits. For the Consequence of Murther is hanging, with which the Rabble is wonderfully delighted. But where Murthers and walking Spirits meet, there is no other Narrative can come neare it.

—SAMUEL BUTLER, *PROSE OBSERVATIONS*

In that real world, the ultimate array of causes of Gulf War syndrome may well include organic agents of the sort already suspected, some military toxin being the most popular candidate; but the cultural contours of the syndrome as it currently manifests itself make it pretty clear that, whatever turns out to have instigated the syndrome, the way Gulf War syndrome has been acted out in the world conforms not only to fin de siècle patterns but to classic patterns of response to the intolerable stresses of war.

We are all familiar with shell shock, battle fatigue, combat neurosis, and post-traumatic stress disorder, and we should realize that their underlying similarity is significant. Our problem has always been that we have tended to treat these conversion responses to the intolerable as forms of malingering. And because we treat them as ultimately imaginary, we cannot conceive that they are caused by agencies fully as significant as any germ. But more important than that, though stemming from the same failure of our human imaginations, we refuse to allow any introduction of "real" organic causation into our understanding of "imaginary" anguish. It's like apples and pears. So when a genuinely complicated phenomenon such as Gulf War syndrome comes along, we are left with an intellectually bankrupt either/or: Either Gulf War syndrome is "real" (that is, rooted in solely organic agents) or it is equivalent to malingering (that is, it reflects nothing but intolerable stress).

If it's organic, blame the government.

If it's "imaginary," blame the victim.

This is millennial thinking.

As more than one thinker has suggested, our human obsession with either/or, he-who-is-not-with-me-is-against-me thinking has a great deal more to do with bilateral symmetry, with the fact that as human beings almost all of us have two sides, than it has to do with the big soup of reality.

Definition

Millennialism: A disease of bilateral symmetry.

It may not be impertinent to suggest, then, that Gulf War syndrome constitutes a realistic response of the human organism to the abstract and surreal nightmarishness of armed combat at the end of this century. For this is a time in which there is no enemy to believe in. There is no combat zone that does not resemble bad movies on television. Personal weapons are now so sophisticated they break down if it rains, and they don't really matter anymore. What really matters is what is *invisible*.

The fear of combat soldiers that they are breathing invisible poison from the air is not entirely dissimilar to the fear of some of the rest of us that we are breathing the last pure oxygen the planet has to offer.

No wonder we break out in rashes and lesions.

Like fish in a drained pond, under a hot sun.

Waiting for the end.

Definition

Apocalypse: A bad air day on Lungfish Beach.

Victims of Gulf War syndrome are certainly not entirely free of the habit of blaming others for what they have done to themselves, a habit of mind cultural critics have frequently found typical of Americans. As a group, however, they are very much less prone to suffer illnesses or experiences that diagnostically depend on there being somebody else at fault than those who experience hysteria in any of the remaining categories suggested by Showalter.

Her next category, for instance, is recovered memory—that is, the process by which "memories" of childhood abuse, almost always against women, are "recovered" from the unconscious depths of the mind. They have reposed there in unreachable darkness—the argument runs—because the original trauma was so severe that all memory of the event has been suppressed. Given the clearly valid feminist presumption that women in general suffer from some form of generalized abuse, it is not difficult to understand the intoxicating neatness of recovered memory as a diagnostic technique. It focuses the argument on the particular. It brings the argument home to every woman.

This universality of application is more or less inevitable, given the nature of the presumed condition. You are deemed to be suffering from childhood sexual abuse trauma by virtue of the fact that whatever symptoms you

may display show no conscious connection to childhood sexual abuse. To refuse to believe that your father or your elder brother or your uncle or your neighbor abused you as a child demonstrates nothing but the strength of the original trauma. The more you refuse today, the more severely you were abused yesterday.

Unfortunately, for many Americans—most of them women—at the end of the century, this circular nonsense is like catnip. It combines profound victimization (every vicious or wrong thing I have done in my life, every failure I have experienced, is *somebody else's fault*—even if, *especially* if, I can't remember a single wrong committed against my person) and the hot flush of scapegoating.

So persuasive for a while was this unfalsifiable but aesthetically satisfying nonsense, and so raveningly self-devouring are the family romance hells created by modern men and women, that legal action was taken against some of the accused abusers. Some went to jail; others were ostracized by their communities. Only at the end of the 1990s has the tide turned in the legal world.

With recovered memory, with the discovery of a scapegoat to blame one's deficiencies as an adult upon, with the naming of names and the placing of places, we begin to approach the mind-set of the millennium.

If you wanted to get America destroyed, if you were a malevolent, evil force, and you said, "**How can I turn God against America?** What can I do to get God mad at the people of America to cause this great land to vomit out the people?" Well, I'd pick five things. I'd begin to have **incest,** I'd begin to commit **adultery** wherever possible. I'd begin to have them offering them up and **killing their babies.** I'd get them having **homosexual** relations and I'd have them having **sex with animals.**

—PAT ROBERTSON

And now we come to satanic ritual abuse, and we've arrived.

We have arrived at a mind-set so inextricably (but at the same time so *shallowly*) troubled, and so poisonous about the sexual nature of human beings, that its examination is something perhaps better left to professionals. To hear someone such as Pat Robertson conflate (say) homosexuality and sex with animals is to eavesdrop on a plea of moral bankruptcy on the part of the Christian religion in a world that has grown enormously in known complexity since ideas of this sort first began to corrupt the minds of Christians. We simply cannot afford the varieties of Pat Robertson in a world that desperately needs to be run by adults.

Americans tend to pussyfoot about the dark underbelly of the American dream, which is its religious right, but out of the unspeakably embarrassing, bestially unloving mind-set of American fundamentalism comes many of the most damaging assumptions about human nature that still poison our understanding of ourselves, and of our relationship to the planet. We mention these issues here without any intention of mounting a sustained analysis of the mind-set

When the United States switches to the public broadcasting service at 9 A.M. it sees the Teletubbies. But fundamentalist preacher Jerry Falwell, the founder of the now defunct Moral Majority, sees a degenerate.

Specifically, he sees Tinky Winky. La La and Po do not play large parts in this theological debate.

"Parents Alert: Tinky Winky Comes Out of the Closet," warns a headline in the latest edition of his *National Liberty Review*, edited and published by the 66-year-old Baptist preacher of Lynchburg, Virginia.

"The character, whose voice is obviously that of a boy, has been found carrying a red purse," writes Dr. Falwell, who does not spend much time in France, "and has become a favorite character among gay groups worldwide.

"Further evidence that the creators of the series intend for Tinky Winky to be a gay role model have surfaced. He is purple—the gay-pride color—and his antenna is shaped like a triangle—the gay-pride symbol."

Dr. Falwell, perhaps choking on a piece of Tubby toast, said yesterday that he believed the "subtle depictions" were intentional. "As a Christian, I feel that role-modeling the gay lifestyle is damaging to the moral lives of children."

—MICHAEL ELLISON

I don't think the human species will ever go extinct. I think we'll find the wisdom to put ourselves on the course of near-infinite tenancy of the earth.

—EDWARD O. WILSON

of men and women who earn salaries by applying professional techniques to create hatred and contempt *for others,* on the behalf of a debased vision of a great religion. But insofar as Pat Robertson and his like speak to anybody stupid enough to believe that fault lies elsewhere, they speak to the kind of people who can count to a thousand and think they have counted to the end of the world.

Sign here for a cut of the guilty.

—THE LITTLE BOOK OF APHORISMS OF THE END

The millennium they anticipate (the millennium in which they are saved and the "guilty" suffer) will never come.

It is nothing but codswallop.

Utterly *incredible* codswallop.

It is one of the stupidest stories ever told.

But the apocalypse—now, that's something else.

The apocalypse anxiety Pat Robertson and his like batten on is very real indeed, and points to the abyss we all face upon this planet we have so mercilessly used as a platform from which to boast to God about the enemies we've destroyed.

And there is no twelve-step program to solve it.

There is no time left.

There is no time to argue with Pat Robertson.

Here is a prediction. It is one of the very few you will find in this book:

Very soon, if the grown-ups don't start to run the world, we're going to be dead.

Satanic ritual abuse (or SRA) is more interesting than those who profit from it. Like most mass hysterias, it grew from an isolated "case" or two (around about 1986) into the paradigmatic Mexican Wave phenomenon of a full-blown "epidemic." It was usually women who reported being victims—of being enlisted in satanic ceremonies, watching as children were tortured and dismembered and burned, being tortured themselves, seeing children being photographed for child pornography rings, et cetera, et cetera. Those who were accused of masterminding the rituals were, however, usually men.

(This is not the place to discuss the strange, sick relationship between children and their parents and others in the Western world of the end times. Suffice it to say that gross sentimentality about children, sometimes approaching Victorian intensity, along with horribly exaggerated fears that sexual trauma may be inflicted upon them go hand in hand—in a classic conversion hysteria scenario—with fear and paralyzed indifference about children's *real* needs. This refusal to pay attention is not simply ideological stupidity; it's not merely some right-wing bee in the vast American bonnet about well-funded schools being sinks of socialist iniquity that explains the radical underfunding of education and the fearful, asinine devaluation of teachers in America. No. Underfunding of education, at the hands of the same prurient ninnies who believe satanic ritual abuse is rampant, is a clear sign of hysteria at work.)

The satanic ritual abuse sickness grew rapidly, and spread outside the borders of the United States. One famous case occurred in the United Kingdom in 1991, in the extremely remote Orkney Islands. During the course of the case—which the British press, to its credit, treated as stinkingly dubious from very early on—nine children were removed—that is, legally abducted—from their families, some of these families being "outsiders" as far as the suffocatingly inbred natives of Orkney were concerned, on the testimony of a single person, who based his accusation on tales told by children, none of whom (to my knowledge) did *not* watch television. In these stories, the abusers were described as wearing costumes that made them look like Ninja Turtles (but no penny dropped in the minds of the social workers involved).

To the contrary, as usual in these cases, the uncanny uniformity of the children's stories was taken to demonstrate the truth of the narrative. Also as usual, the similarity of these stories to preexisting horror films—to a whole *genre* of satanic ritual abuse horror stories—was dismissed. The traumatized families eventually got their children back, and the social workers were chastised, but the human cost of this exercise in practical Christianity was higher than the cost to the entire world (or to any individual at all) if every single one of Pat Robertson's contemptible litany of Sins God Should End the World Because Of were committed, simultaneously, on live television, in Times Square. The only "sin" one might continue to condemn would, perhaps, be incest in an inbred island community already saturated by faith.

In the end, of course, it is the same with satanic ritual abuse as it is with millennialism.

It is nonsense. It is a vastation of nonsense. It leads sane men and women to despair of our race as we hurtle down the long chute into the next century, where genuine challenges meet us, challenges that we must meet in turn, or else. Or else the likes of Pat Robertson get their way.

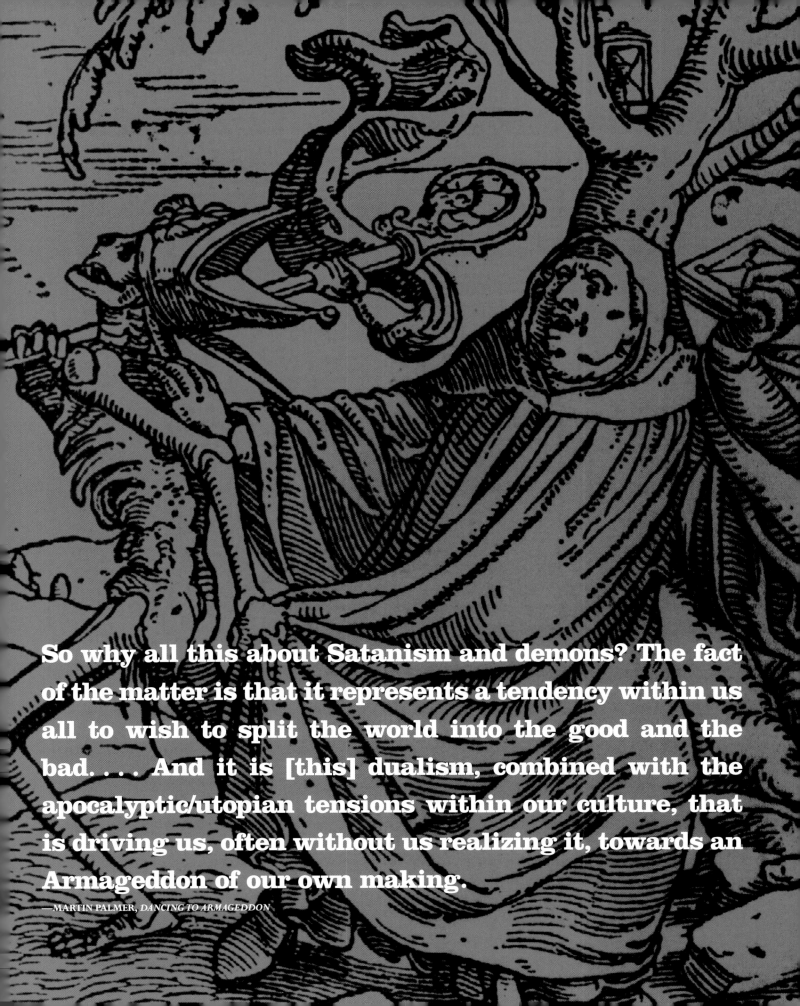

So why all this about Satanism and demons? The fact of the matter is that it represents a tendency within us all to wish to split the world into the good and the bad. . . . And it is [this] dualism, combined with the apocalyptic/utopian tensions within our culture, that is driving us, often without us realizing it, towards an Armageddon of our own making.

—MARTIN PALMER, *DANCING TO ARMAGEDDON*

By the way: Despite the vast amount of apparatus needed to *do* a good satanic ritual, and the large crews of heavily costumed extras required to make the thing convincing, and the sheer *noisiness* of the abominations so solicitously listed and described by the religious right, and the extensive police investigations that have been undertaken to track down abusers, no evidence of any satanic ritual abuse has ever been uncovered.

This is because it doesn't exist.

"I only wish *I* had such eyes," the King remarked in a fretful tone. "To be able to see Nobody! And at *that* distance too! Why, it's as much as *I* can do to see real people, by this light!"

—LEWIS CARROLL, *THROUGH THE LOOKING GLASS*

Ah, but.

The fundamentalist right does have a rejoinder, of course, one so constructed that the more it is refuted the stronger it gets, like Antaeus.

No evidence? runs the rejoinder. *Don't you see? That proves it! Only Satan himself could leave no evidence at all! It's a conspiracy!*

Satanic ritual abuse did not only serve as a hysterical displacement for undereducated social workers floundering in the psychic bogs of the *fin de millénium* where the center does not hold and children spit upon the winding gyre that brings the million dread tomorrows down; as Showalter makes clear, it also served the likes of Professor Cory Hammond of the University of Utah medical school, upon whom she spends some valuable time.

Hammond argues that satanic cults are part of a Nazi conspiracy, one led (conveniently, as he has a lot of anti-Semitic material to impart) by a renegade Jew who heads a secret organization. (The alarm bells begin to ring. There have been a large number of World War II fantasies published over the past twenty or so years that show the Nazi hierarchy to be in league with Satan; in some of these novels, a secret cadre of satanic Nazis survives the war and works to corrupt decent Americans at home and play.) Hammond's Jew's name is Green. He is a specialist in brainwashing and stuff. His satanic cults are designed to create "tens of thousands of mental robots who will do pornography," et cetera, et cetera.

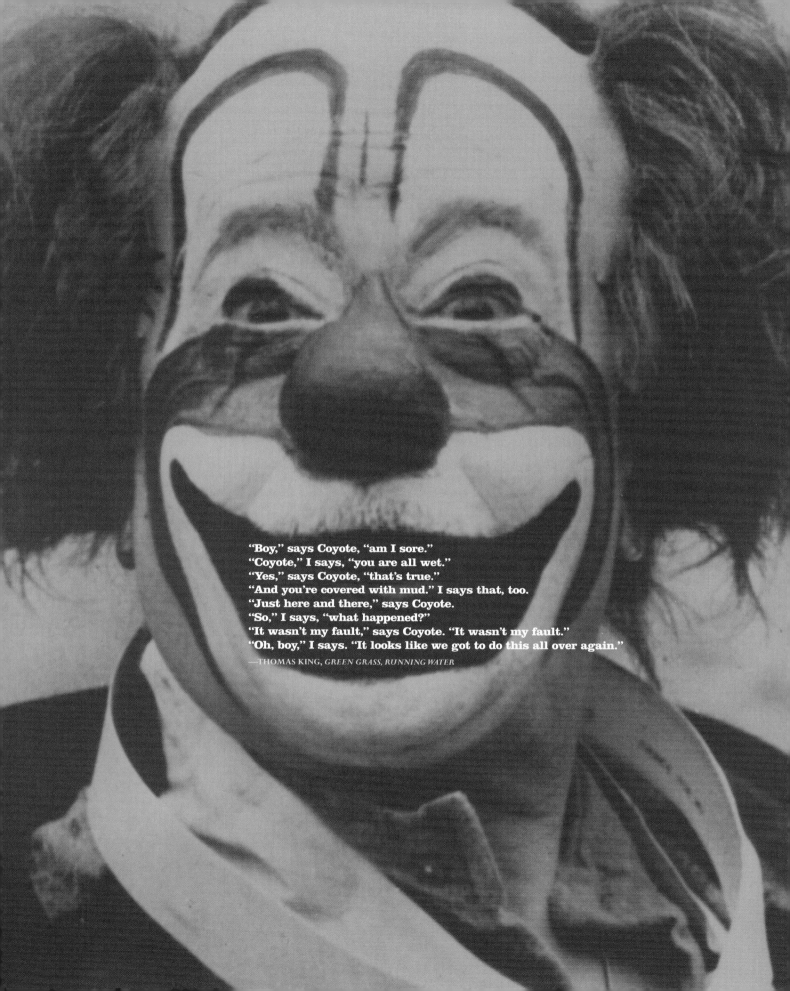

"Boy," says Coyote, "am I sore."
"Coyote," I says, "you are all wet."
"Yes," says Coyote, "that's true."
"And you're covered with mud." I says that, too.
"Just here and there," says Coyote.
"So," I says, "what happened?"
"It wasn't my fault," says Coyote. "It wasn't my fault."
"Oh, boy," I says. "It looks like we got to do this all over again."
—THOMAS KING, *GREEN GRASS, RUNNING WATER*

Children—your children and mine!—are programmed by Green's Nazi goons from the age of two, through the use of electrical shocks and drugs such as Demerol, and their personalities are secretly transformed, so that even their parents do not know that they are raising little devils. Therefore, no matter what you do to your child through stupidity or malice, *it's not your fault*. No matter that they act out your own hysteria like little robots of the family romance. No matter if they borrow the guns you polish with spit and prayers, and mow down their classmates with the live bullets you've left on the mantel; it's not your fault. They are not you. They do not carry your awful inadequacy as a human being into the millennium. Whatever they are is because of *them*. They were turned into aliens—Midwich Cuckoos—by someone else.

Here is Professor Hammond on the various programs that are inflicted on our children by satanists, from Alpha on down:

Alpha represents general programming. Beta appears to be sexual programs, such as how to perform oral sex in a certain way or how to produce and direct child pornography films or run child prostitution rings. Delta are killers. Delta-alters are trained to kill in ceremonies and also do some self-harm stuff. Theta are psychic killers. This comes from their belief in psychic abilities including their belief that they can make someone develop a brain tumor and die. Omega are self-destruct programs which can make the patient self-mutilate or kill themselves. . . .

And so on.

We do not quote Professor Hammond at length from simple spite, though it is always possible to hope that if enough sane people read him, he will be laughed into early retirement. We quote him to underline something about those grown men and women who believe—we must remember—not only in the nonfact that people perform rituals intended to evoke Satan, and in the course of which children are tortured and sexually abused; they also believe that Satan and/or his minions are actually present in these rituals. We quote Professor Hammond to give some sense of the extremity of not-seeing that must stain the souls of those who do read him—and the other writers like him who generate excuses for our own oceanic unappeasable guilts—and believe what they read.

There is a lot they do not see.

They do not see the absence of Satan from this world.

They do not see that it is monstrous to accuse other human beings of participating in horsefeather confabulations such as satanic ritual abuse.

They do not see their children.

That is perhaps the most important not-seeing of all.

They do not see their children, because to see their children as they are, they risk seeing themselves. It is this risk that Dr. Morbius (Walter Pidgeon)—the Prospero figure in Fred Wilcox's film *Forbidden Planet* (1956)—attempts to avoid when he refuses to understand that the "monster" draining his strength and threatening to destroy everyone else is not an objective creature at all but his own Caliban Id. He himself is the ravening Evil Twin who attacks from within.

I keep coming back to its central conceit: the idea that technology gives us the power to facilitate our own inner violence, to make our dreams dangerously real. We have the power to destroy ourselves, the film suggests, only when our own unconscious wishes and fears are sent into the world. When, indeed, they *become* the world—a tissue of irrational fears, a screen onto which we project our various phobias and desires. "The first world we find outside is, in part, a repository for the terror inside us, an elsewhere for those desires and objects that bring unpleasure," the psychoanalyst Adam Phillips writes in his book *On Kissing, Tickling, and Being Bored* (1993). "And that world we make outside is the world we need to get away from. It is the place, or one of the places, where we put the objects and desires we wish did not belong to us. To be at home in the world we need to keep it inhospitable."

The cultural world is very much a construction of our dreams, those that express wishes but also those that give shape to our deepest terrors—visions of utopias but also of apocalypse. . . . Nobody invented the apocalyptic facts of our end-of-millennium culture—free-falling economies, drastic overpopulation, wars and famines—but our projections of imagination onto these vents (phantasies, in Freudian usage) express at least as much about the state of the world as they do about our desires and wishes for that world.

—MARK KINGWELL, *DREAMS OF MILLENNIUM*

The extraordinary viciousness—the malarial inexpugnancy—of the mind-set that sees Satan in other people's homes is an exudation of hysteria. It is the hysteria of a person whose psyche is as rigid as a cockroach's carapace, the psyche of a person who cannot for the life of him see that life is what the mirror says.

We are very close to the hysteria of millennium—the hysteria that acts out, but fails to metabolize, our apocalyptic intuitions. For the millennium is the hysteria of the Western world at bay.

I knew I had to keep myself tidy for what lay ahead.

—DIANA, PRINCESS OF WALES, ON BEING ASKED ABOUT HER PREMARITAL VIRGINITY

It was difficult to irritate Satan, but that accomplished it.

"What an ass you are!" he said. "Are you so unobservant as not to have found out that sanity and happiness are an impossible combination? No sane man can be happy, for to him life is real, and he sees what a fearful thing it is. Only the mad can be happy, and not many of those. The few that imagine themselves kings or gods are happy, the rest are no happier than the sane."

—MARK TWAIN, *THE MYSTERIOUS STRANGER*

ABDUCT ME OUTTA THIS!

After chronic fatigue syndrome, Gulf War syndrome, recovered memory, and satanic ritual abuse, there was only one way to go: into the ether, into the sublime.

Showalter wrote too soon to have responded to mobile phone stigmata syndrome, or MPSS, but not too soon to have had a chance to think about a very obvious climax, which is alien abduction; it is perhaps the most "sentimental" of all hysterias,

"Sentimentalists," says the PILGRIM's SCRIP, "are they who seek to enjoy Reality, without incurring the Immense Debtorship for a thing done."

—GEORGE MEREDITH, *THE ORDEAL OF RICHARD FEVEREL*

though sentimentality is a characteristic of almost any hysteria: It is inherently easier on the sufferer than reality. Hysterics are they who seek to enjoy reality without incurring the Immense Debtorship for a thing done: which is to say, hysterics act out faked realities in order to avoid the cost of metabolizing the real thing.

Roswell is a small town in southeastern New Mexico. Before 1947 it was not remarkable for anything in particular. Since then, what "happened" in Roswell in 1947 has gradually acquired the patina of mysteriously archaic authenticity that in America adheres only to events that occurred before 1956, when color television was introduced.

(For children today, and for many of their parents, there are two kinds of past: yesterday, which is in color; and history, or "ago," which is in black and white. The convention by which historical events need the authentication of black-and-white registration is so powerful that—for instance—the events surrounding the death of John F. Kennedy are very frequently rendered in black and white, whether or not the original footage or camera work was shot in color.

Roswell is real because it is not in color.)

The premise of *Timequake One* was that a timequake, a sudden glitch in the space-time continuum, made everybody and everything do exactly what they'd done during a past decade, for good or ill, a second time. It was déjà vu that wouldn't quit for ten long years. . . .

There was absolutely nothing you could say during the rerun, if you hadn't said it the first time through the decade. You couldn't even save your own life or that of a loved one, if you had failed to do that the first time through.

I had the timequake zap everybody and everything in an instant from February 13th, 2001, back to February 17th, 1991. Then we all had to get back to 2001 the hard way, minute by minute, hour by hour, year by year, betting on the wrong horse again, marrying the wrong person again, getting the clap again.

You name it!

—KURT VONNEGUT, *TIMEQUAKE*

It is very difficult in most western societies to express pain or distress openly; we seem to have almost forgotten how to mourn or to share suffering without the help of "experts." We assume that we have the "right" to be happy. Yet we rarely are, and happiness anyway is a feeling, not a possession. Thus we have tried to package the "happiness" thing into social programmes or specific products. The occurrence of distress, sadness, suffering, or any of the other emotions which are not "happy" is seen as the intrusion of something foreign, rather than as a normal part of life. These emotions and feelings thus become deeply disturbing and we seek to smother them, rather than see them as part and parcel of the variety of life. The Pursuit of Happiness is a belief that utopia is around us and we can be part of it if only we have the money, the right goods, contacts, time, or the correct outlook.

—MARTIN PALMER, *DANCING TO ARMAGEDDON*

Nineteen forty-seven, in any case, was a remarkable year. After the infernal toggle of the A-bomb just eighteen months earlier, 1947 turned out to be a year in which the course of world history began to feed into a new arena: the Cold War. It began to sink in upon Americans that whatever was happening in the world now—just when the Cold War began to gain momentum, when the rosy glow of the bomb that would end war turned into an infernal grin and the Western world began to realize that something truly apocalyptic had been unleashed—if one was able to look straight into the mirror and tell the truth about what one saw there, we had opened the infernal door ourselves.

But it is not easy for most of us—certainly it is not easy for Americans, notorious as they are for their sense of entitlement, and for their compulsive tendency to blame someone else or the government or God for everything that goes wrong in their world—it is not easy, it is terribly hard, to take responsibility for something like the A-bomb.

It may be that in 1999 we no longer worry very much about nuclear holocaust because the world has changed so enormously since the fall of the Soviet Union, and because—after all—we're still here, and so is the world. (Later we will touch on how fragile that security really is when looked at soberly, as 2000 nears.) But in 1947 the fear of nuclear holocaust was a new thing, and the anxiety it generated was both nightmare-vivid and pressing; and it's almost certainly no coincidence that it was just then that UFOs—whose presence conveniently absolves the human race of any real responsibility for *anything*—began to perform their pancake flip-flops through Western skies.

What a relief they must have been. Especially as most of us, even then, knew in our hearts how terribly unlikely it was that UFOs actually did exist. Science fiction writers from 1926 on had been longing for first contact with a genuine alien species and had been writing stories embodying this great dream for decades, but not a single one of them believed for an instant that the UFO phenomenon represented anything more than wish fulfillment. There was a luxury in this for sf writers, of course: the luxury of pretending to believe in something that won't threaten us by coming true.

The fundamental problem with UFOs—over and above the fact that they do not exist—and the later phenomenon of and craze for "alien abductions" is the thinness of the story of the world they generate. They replace the murmurous hugeness of the experience of being human on this planet with a fantasy that is mechanical, paranoid, trivial, and boring: that cartoon aliens are so obsessed by human beings that they secretly come trillions upon trillions of miles in saucers to our planet in order to find out what's inside humanity's bodily orifices, and to inflict cunning false-memory syndrome on their victims.

All the same, Roswell itself has become a typical focus or releaser for the anxiety plagues that increasingly afflict the human race so globally that theories of alien visitation seem to have a placebo effect for a lucky few million.

What happened at Roswell? Most scientists say that nothing happened. Nothing at all out of the ordinary. Maybe some of the highly secretive, paranoia-inducing military activity that was so common everywhere in the Cold War period. True believers, on the other hand, claim that extraterrestrials in flying saucers landed there sometime in July 1947, that some or all of these visitors were injured, that the federal government covered up what happened from the very beginning of this most important event in human history, and that half a century later the government is still concealing the truth.

It is not our purpose in *The Book of End Times* to deliver a final verdict on Roswell, or upon any other event or nonevent of similar symbolic importance (although my own opinions on the matter are clear enough). We are more interested in the reason a story exists than in its facticity. In any case, when dealing with true believers, it is wise always to remember that for them it is the belief that runs the show, not the show that creates the belief. True belief is omnivorous: Any scraps will do. If UFOs become impossible to talk about with a straight face, then the true believer—like those who believe in the millennium but keep on getting the dates wrong—will simply pick upon some new, ludicrous, obnoxiously dumb idea to expatiate on.

But it *is* our purpose to say why civilization at the end of the twentieth century demands stories like Roswell, whose *story*—the story of alien landings, of total submission to sexual probings out of our universal stock of forbidden fantasies, of a conspiracy of silence, of a race of wise mentors that has been prevented from saving us all—makes so much better telling than the government version of events, whose incoherence reeks, to the cynical mind, of the chaos of unsorted reality. For many of us—perhaps for most of us—it is sadly the case that we can believe only what we can be told.

This is the basic conspiracy as thus far revealed within the show, as noted chronologically. At some point during the Second World War it was discovered that aliens are visiting the earth. We the viewers do not yet know if these **aliens are benevolent or malevolent,** although slowly but surely the hints are tending to favor the former. After the end of the war several crashed ships were recovered, and at that point the conspiracy began getting under way. Those who put together the basic conspiracy appear to have been a small group of older men who are already in charge of the basic conspiracy that runs the world, **politically and financially.** With their government connections—generally, again apparently, involved in each country's intelligence ministries and agencies—they set scientists to studying the ships and

aliens. These scientists included Americans as well as Nazis and Japanese, the latter two groups being the ones who (as far as we presently know) set about attempting to create human-alien hybrids. The Americans included, among others, Mulder's father. At one point, for reasons as yet fully unknown, he has to offer one of his two children as a subject to—aliens? Humans? It's fuzzy. At first he plans to give over Mulder, but then instead gives over Mulder's younger sister. Mulder, as a child, **sees her abducted by a UFO from the living room** of their house, which sets him off in his search to find the truth about what's going on, and his search to find his sister (she may, or may not, be dead).

In the meantime, in the bigger picture, other arrangements and pacts would appear, possibly, to have been made between aliens and humans; certainly

aliens have been continuing to visit. One of the many unanswered questions thus far is how much of what people see as UFO-related activity **is in truth produced by government agencies,** deliberately or inadvertently.

By the time of the show's action, the basic setup is that a shadowy cabal within the U.S. government (and in league with the international cabal) essentially is able to hold complete power over all other agencies, and has killed anyone who attempts to discover, or begins to discover, the truth. **The CIA would seem to be involved—certainly more so than the FBI,** which is basically powerless in the face of these characters—but not always. There are layers upon layers upon layers of intrigue. Characters who have seemed trustworthy may or may not be; characters who have been terribly evil aren't, always. **M[ulder] & S[cully] can never be sure—they can trust each other, but no one else; usually.**

Trying to write down even the basics of this make me realize how astonishingly complex they've managed to get it by this point. The remarkable thing is that thus far they've been able to hold, entirely, to an absolutely coherent context for all of it, and one ready (as in any conspiracy theory) to be infinitely expanded. Carter, the creator, came up with the basics (and a lot of it has been, I think, almost unconsciously done on his part; he's been working off a lot of the **subconscious reptile-brain fears** of the average American, and that's why this stuff always comes across as unnervingly believable); and since Duchovny has been writing the conspiracy episodes with him, or at least coming up with a lot of the basic ideas, the thing has gotten (as you noted) more heavily layered. They're working with intensely powerful material here and at times come up with **some really nasty implications.**

—JACK WOMACK

The story of Roswell is a winner: the haunted photographs; the guilt-ridden faces of officialdom; the distorted, alienlike countenances of wounded pilots; the laborious prevarications; the dream of an answer from the stars; the absolute conviction that the dizzyingly complex world we now live in, which is so incomprehensible to us, couldn't just have happened. That somebody must have made it up. That none of it is our doing. That none of it is our fault.

As we enter deeper and deeper into the end times, we find ourselves consorting more and more with fellow citizens of the world who do not share *Life*'s abject sense that the human story has now been told, or the *Observer*'s feeling that if there is a story, it is simply too much to deal with. Increasingly, another reaction to the end times is coming to the fore. It is the feeling, on the part of many of us, that not only was the world made up in the first place, probably by God, but something or someone has *betrayed* what was intended. That we are not simply victims of the way of the world: that we are, in fact, persecuted.

Some of us who feel this way sit at home and bitch about the government.

Some of us join churches and await the Rapture, because we have come to believe that the great betrayal is the first (or second, or umpteenth) act in a vast millennial drama distilled out of selected chapters of *The Revelation of St. John the Divine.*

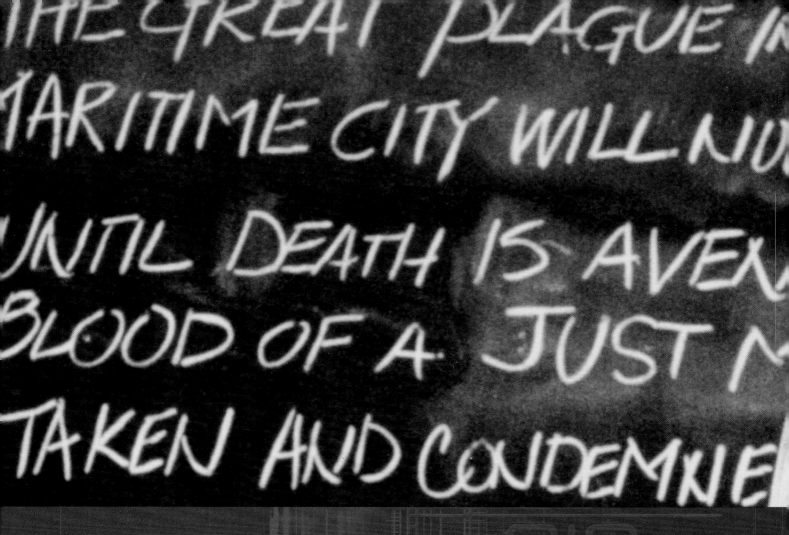

THE GREAT PLAGUE IN
MARITIME CITY WILL NOT
UNTIL DEATH IS AVEN
BLOOD OF A JUST N
TAKEN AND CONDEMNE

Some of us are abducted by aliens. At least *they* care.

Some of us—triggered into action by overwhelming forebodings beyond the daylight mind's ability to make sense of things, or personal inadequacies and resentments, or tragedies too grim to comprehend—enter into the ceremonies of killing—the Wacos, the black trench coats at Columbine High School—that have become a highlighted feature of century's end.

In the book "Finding the Heart of the Child," the psychiatrist Edward Hallowell cogently lists many of the factors that contribute to the kind of alienation that allows something like Littleton to occur. These include changing family structure (single-parent homes, two-career homes); the breakdown of communities, villages and neighborhoods; cynicism about government and social institutions; the decrease in a sense of security, job permanence or close personal relationships; the decline of genuine spirituality as an ethical force in the culture; an explosion of information that creates anxiety over one's worth or abilities; a lack of respect for older people and an overreliance on "self" to find the meaning of life.
—GARY ROSS

There are, perhaps, fewer random killings than we are inclined to believe.

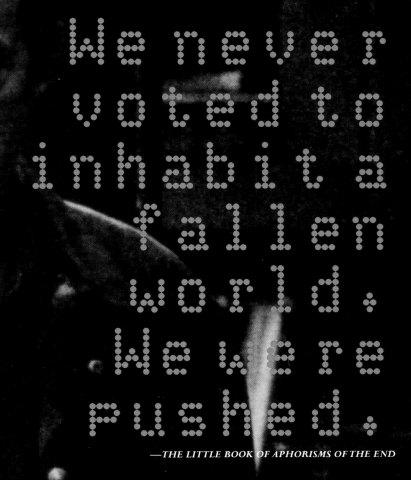

We never voted to inhabit a fallen world: We were pushed.

—*THE LITTLE BOOK OF APHORISMS OF THE END*

Human beings kill for a reason—almost always a despicable reason.

It is possible that some otherwise inexplicable killings have been motivated by some inchoate but irresistible desire to trigger the end times.

To get the story going.

To allay dread anxieties over losing control by taking the story into one's own hands.

Killers of this sort, for instance, were featured again and again in *Millennium,* a fictional TV series created by Chris Carter (who had earlier created *The X-Files*). The protagonist of this series was an ex-FBI agent named Frank Black, who lived (in the first two seasons) on Ezekiel Drive in Seattle, and who had a paranormal ability to enter into the minds or mind-sets of serial killers who had been triggered by some darkness up ahead—killers who knew or thought they knew something we didn't perceive, but which Black and the Millennium Group (which Black alternately belongs to and battles against) suspected may have been there.

Lost in a world that betrayed them—perhaps simply by being too complex, too unknowable to tolerate, too full of trick-ster boundary lines, and too empty of homesteads—they fell into the belief or delusion that actions could somehow create around them an arena of meaning.

I remember you

when I have heard you the soles of my feet have made answer
when I have seen you I have waked and slipped from the calendars
from the creeds of difference and the contradictions
that were my life and all the crumbling fabrications
as long as it lasted until something that we were
had ended when you are no longer anything
let me catch sight of you again going over the wall
and before the garden is extinct and the woods are figures
guttering on a screen let my words find their own
places in the silence after the animals

—W. S. MERWIN , "VIXEN"

The delusion includes the idea that to do something is to create a dramatic context within which one's actions mean some-thing; that to do something is to have an audience who shares your sense of what's happening; and that to do more than one action in a row is to have a script (for modern millenarians that script almost certainly comes out of *The Revelation of St. John the Divine*). And what better script could one imagine than a tale from Revelation? Because the whole world will be the arena,

The carnivalesque marketplace depicted in modern literature will be far different from the idealized image of a boisterous medieval fair or even from the safe confines of Diderot's Café de la Régence. Instead, the reader will follow an itinerary through a continent in ruins, in which insane murderers and shell-shocked victims stagger from one bombed-out castle to another. The most fitting slogan for this apocalyptic carnival is Céline's outcry toward the end of *Rigodon*: "That's what man has come to with all his immense, ecumenical, super-atomic progress: everybody's in the arena and not a single spectator is left in the stands."

—MICHAEL ANDRÉ BERNSTEIN, *BITTER CARNIVAL*

the whole world will be at stake.

From somewhere up ahead, there is a sound of hoofbeats.

The world is a chess-board. What strange and complicated games are transacted upon it! All men are players, moving respectively, and in the civil, religious and political scenes

continue thus to do, until the automaton DEATH, with his eyeless skull and fleshless hand, stalks before, chattering with his ghastly jaws, "*check-mate!*"

—KIT KELVIN , *KERNELS*

Actual Dream of the Second Coming, Roger Brown

THERE IS A WASTELAND

Part Three

and it is us

The old Northern faith contained the fearsome doctrine of the Dusk of the Gods. In our days there have arisen in more highly-developed minds vague qualms of a Dusk of the Nations, in which all suns and all stars are gradually waning, and mankind with all its institutions and creations is perishing in the midst of a dying world.

—MAX NORDAU, *DEGENERATION*

Turning and turning in the widening gyre
The falcon cannot hear the falconer;
Things fall apart; the centre cannot hold;
Mere anarchy is loosed upon the world,
The blood-dimmed tide is loosed, and everywhere
The ceremony of innocence is drowned;
The best lack all conviction, while the worst
Are full of passionate intensity.

Surely some revelation is at hand;
Surely the Second Coming is at hand.
The Second Coming! Hardly are those words out
When a vast image out of *Spiritus Mundi*
Troubles my sight: somewhere in sands of the desert
A shape with lion body and the head of a man,
A gaze blank and pitiless as the sun,
Is moving its slow thighs, while all about it
Reel shadows of the indignant desert birds.
The darkness drops again; but now I know
That twenty centuries of stony sleep
Were vexed to nightmare by a rocking cradle,
And what rough beast, its hour come round at last,
Slouches towards Bethlehem to be born?

—WILLIAM BUTLER YEATS, "THE SECOND COMING"

But oh, **beamish nephew,** beware of the day,
If your Snark be a Boojum! For then
You will softly and suddenly vanish away,
And never be met with again!

—LEWIS CARROLL, *THE HUNTING OF THE SNARK*

A CAST OF CHARACTERS

And here we slam against the buffers, we run into the stone wall. We have been wandering up and down the anxious planet for symptoms and symbols of apocalypse, and we have found ample signs of premonition, malaise, and self-knowledge and its bad twin, hysteria. We have also found that many of us have shared a very public sense that the end of the century is a convenient milestone—a tollbooth manned by Hermes in trickster motley—where we can pause in order to gain some perspective on the course our fellow sophists have taken up to now, and on our thousand courses hence. But now we must glance for a moment at some of those who, rather than balancing in the wind of time, have turned their backs on the future and created the millennium.

The millennium is, of course, nothing at all but a number. So we can call it any number of things.

We can call it a vacuum. Or a cocoon. Or a cardboard mask painted with a silly face. Whatever we call this thing of the mind, it keeps us from seeing the true face of apocalypse. It is the mask the *Observer* editors fixed over the countenance of Dr. Hooke. It is the mask of hysteria. When we look into the mirror and see a Tamagotchi face opening its mouth to squall, we are looking pastward into a mask. The millennium itself—in all the celebratory hype being prepared to usher it onstage, in the stadiums and Disneyfied Times Square theme parks being erected to sell it to us, in the fatuous prognostications of a thousand thousand merchandisers of avoidance—is, as we have said, Tamagotchi. It is a contraption of architecture and hype and thought that requires our hysterical attention in order to function.

The tragic, self-destructive, poisonous villains, serial killers, self-mutilators, and agents of the devil who populate the first several episodes of the Chris Carter TV series *Millennium* seem awash in a world from which meaning has been drained, leaving them nothing but base desires and unforgivable obsessions. They are, all of them, potential victims of the creators of millennialism, as they search for a story that will explain to them the horror, the blackness they feel inside—and justify their actions to others. The Millennium Group itself, which began as a shadowy paternal protecting organization opposed to the fanatics who create story-viruses to infect the weak, now seems in 1999 to be, shockingly, yet another fomenter of some numerological version of the end of things.

To ignore the millennium, and to face the apocalypse, would require us to strip ourselves naked of our hysterias and to face forward.

And then to grapple.

All the same, when we hear the Horsemen in our dreams, we can understand the need for a millennium story, understand the huge potency of the millennium as a climax in the story of our times. The story of the millennium is a way to escape telling ourselves how it has all gone wrong, by virtue of the fact that (as we've already claimed) it is a displacement device designed to keep us from understanding that we have already met the future and the future is us. The millennium story takes us away from the given and the secular, and it suggests to the needy and the vicious who absorb the story that we never need return there.

A huge amount has been written about millennialists. Unfortunately, most of the books about people who guess wrong about the millennium, or about other similar events, are written by authors who secretly—sometimes not so secretly—think they must have somehow been *right*. Litanies of special pleading about appalling wrong-guessers such as, for instance, Nostradamus, proliferate. It is possible to be sympathetic without hanging rationality out to twist in the wind, but it is not frequently done.

It is our heritage, however, and we must make a nod to it. Many of the books published on millennial thinking and on the millennium itself have devoted most of their pages—one can only imagine the ardor of authors bound to the wheel of exposition of this stuff—to the analysis, sometimes gullibly expressed, sometimes acerbic, of this sad underside of the Western mind at work. Here are a couple of examples from the back streets of the West.

GERBERT (c.945–1003)

The man who became Pope Sylvester II just in time to usher in the first millennium. "Tradition," says Stephen Skinner in *Millennium Prophecies* (1994), which is one of many books on the general subject, "has it that he was an advanced student of the black arts, which he first learnt during three years in residence at certain Arabic schools in Spain. It was said he regularly conversed with the Devil, and was even thought by some Cardinals to be the cloven-footed Devil himself." On the night of 31 December 999, Gerbert celebrated mass. Afterward there was silence. There are rumors it was a dread silence. Then it was 1000. That is the sum of what happened.

We do not refer to Stephen Skinner maliciously, in order to single him out, but solely for convenience. The pattern of his ruminations and the bent of his scholarship are typical of the field in general. Anything we might imply about the quality of his work could be said about a hundred—a thousand—other beavers in this particular pond.

That night your great guns, unawares,
Shook all our coffins as we lay,
And broke the chancel window-squares,
We thought it was the Judgment-day

And sat upright. While drearisome
Arose the howl of wakened hounds:
The mouse let fall the altar-crumb,
The worms drew back into the mounds,

The glebe cow drooled. Till God called, "No;
It's gunnery practice out at sea
Just as before you went below;
The world is as it used to be:

"All nations striving strong to make
Red war yet redder. Mad as hatters
They do no more for Christés sake
Than you who are helpless in such matters.

"That this is not the judgment-hour
For some of them's a blessed thing,
For if it were they'd have to scour
Hell's floor for so much threatening. . . .

"Ha, ha. It will be warmer when
I blow the trumpet (if indeed
I ever do; for you are men,
And rest eternal sorely need)."

So down we lay again. "I wonder,
Will the world ever saner be,"
Said one, "than when He sent us under
In our indifferent century!"

And many a skeleton shook his head.
"Instead of preaching forty year,"
My neighbour Parson Thirdly said,
"I wish I had stuck to pipes and beer."

Again the guns disturbed the hour,
Roaring their readiness to avenge,
As far inland as Stourton Tower,
And Camelot, and starlit Stonehenge.

—THOMAS HARDY, "CHANNEL FIRING"

TRITHEMIUS (1462–1516)

A mysterious kind of guy. He spoke with angels, and sent long messages great distances instantly—"almost four centuries," Stephen Skinner sagaciously emphasizes, "before the invention of the telephone." He caused the Emperor Maximilian in 1482 to have a vision in which his dead wife appeared, complete down to a conspicuous wart on her neck: from then on the Emperor believed Trithemius's word. He told Maximilian the entire history of the world, past, present, and future; he told it in a book. There are various ages. That of the Angel Gabriel extends from 1525 to 1879, when the Angel Michael takes over. At the end of the reign, in the year 2233, the world ends, after having taken the Millennium within its sway. Skinner on the significance of Michael:

It is as if Christ is to return to complete the work he began when he was on earth. Interestingly, Communist stalwarts Joseph Stalin and Leon Trotsky were both born in 1879, the beginning of the Age of the Sun.

So, for that matter, was James Branch Cabell, the author of *Jurgen* (1919), born in 1879; so were John Erskine and Norman Lindsay, both authors of bawdy attacks on traditional Christianity; so was E. M. Forster, a notorious homosexual whose motto—"Only connect"—has become a rallying cry for drug abusers everywhere; so was Vachel Lindsay, who introduced the rhythms of the Congo to American schoolchildren. Some politicians were also born in 1879.

NOSTRADAMUS (1503–1566)

The biggest farce of all. He was the author of *Centuries,* a sequence of approximately a thousand "prophetic" quatrains covering the period 1555–3797, a work that stands at the center of the prophetic tradition, in the sense that a shell game stands at the center of a carnival. At the latter date—3797—the world ends. Nostradamus's calculations were complex, involving astrology, a brazen tripod, astronomy, and high levels of nocturnal stress. These calculations, we are told, were very exact, but Nostradamus, Skinner confirms, "would deliberately avoid including the relevant date for an event in his quatrains, even though this would have been possible."

But not to worry. Many commentators have deciphered the codes by which Nostradamus concealed his exact calculations. These various decipherments, not unnaturally, generate various interpretations of the quatrains, at least one of them (Skinner's) being based on the fact that many of Nostradamus's calculations worked out to be in fairly close proximity to multiples of sixty.

For instance, if one adds 60 to 1606, which Nostradamus had identified as an important year to base predictions on, we get the year 1666 (one millennium plus the number of the Beast). If one adds 60 to 1666, 1726 comes up, which is just one year short of 1727, a year Nostradamus specifically mentions:

The third climate included under Aries;
In the year 1727 in October:
The King of Persia will be captured by those of Egypt:
Battle, death, loss; a great shame to the cross.

When this quatrain mentions Egypt, it means Turkey (Egypt "symbolizes" Turkey). When it mentions war and death and a humiliation to Christianity, it means that a *peace* is concluded between Turkey (here known as Egypt) and Persia. After these necessary special understandings are applied to the quatrain, it becomes very accurate, say scholars in the field.

Here is another date (specific dates are rare in Nostradamus, even though—his followers claim—he *could* have put them all in if he'd *wanted* to):

The year 1999, seventh month,
From the sky will come a great King of Terror:
To bring back to life the great King of the Mongols,
Before and after Mars reigns.

It is commonly agreed that if the great King of the Mongols cannot plausibly be identified with Elvis Presley, then it is perfectly clear that Nostradamus was referring either to the Antichrist, or to Genghis Khan, or to Mao Zedong, or to some other figure.

Archangels Michael & Gabriel, 10th or 11th century

JOANNA SOUTHCOTT (1750–1814)

She gave up men for church when she was forty. She founded her first Southcottian Chapel at the age of fifty or so. She became pregnant with the Messiah at the age of sixty-four, but died. She left behind her a box, which may be opened only in the presence of all twenty-four bishops of the Church of England. All the evidence suggests that it contains world peace, happiness, and the secret of the millennium. A researcher named Harry Price—he was famous for psychical investigations—reportedly opened the box as long ago as 1927, discovering inside "an old nightcap, a flintlock pistol, some papers and a few odds and ends." His investigation has been thoroughly discounted by members of the Panacea Society, founded to preserve Joanna Southcott's vision. The society also preserves the box somewhere in southern England, and expects to open it at the appropriate time.

Michael Shermer, in his fascinating (if King Canute–like) attempt to import reason into modern American belief systems, a book he calls *Why People Believe Weird Things: Pseudoscience, Superstition, and Other Confusions of Our Time* (1997), generates at one point a list of twenty-five fallacious ways of thinking that allow "thinkers" to arrive at the goals they wish to arrive at. Before he begins he instances a maxim of Hume (from the 1748 work *Philosophical Essays Concerning Human Understanding*): "That no testimony is sufficient to establish a miracle, unless the testimony be of such a kind, that its falsehood would be more miraculous than the fact which it endeavors to establish."

As Hume says a little later on, in explanation of this maxim: "Reject the greater miracle."

Hume's maxim has been in the world for 250 years.

It has, of course, been universally ignored.

Shermer's twenty-five points are themselves devastating. Those most relevant to the present concerns include:

1. Theory influences observations.
3. Equipment constructs results.
4. Anecdotes do not make a science.
5. Scientific language does not make a science.
6. Bold statements do not make claims true.
7. Heresy does not equal correctness.
9. Rumors do not equal reality.
10. Unexplained is not inexplicable.

If there is one thing we may be sure of, however, it is that Shermer's twenty-five points will have about as much effect as Hume's maxim on the generality of true believers. The West is brimming full of the stuff of dreams. It is as though we all lived in one of those mythical soups that are never exhausted, because every day the cook adds more ingredients, but never change, because the ingredients all boil down to the same basement broth. And the same figures emerge, under different names, to stain our dreams: Charles Manson, Ted Bundy, Jeffrey Dahmer, David Koresh, John Wayne Gacy, Timothy McVeigh—the serial killers, the mass murderers, the exterminators, the false messiahs. It may be a cheap shot to call them all one person, but in the alembic of nightmare they wear one face.

When your Daemon is in charge,
do not try to think consciously.
Drift, wait, and obey.

—RUDYARD KIPLING, *SOMETHING OF MYSELF*

This horde of abominations with one face may, nowadays, claim to display a gladiator's stoic mien and to fulfill a gladiator's pierced vulnerability (as Timothy McVeigh, "smiling and showing no emotion" as he entered the courtroom to hear that he had been found guilty of the Oklahoma City bombing, which killed 168 people, must have thought himself to be), but a gladiator in what kind of arena, in collusion with what kind of God? He may seem to be a gladiator on the model of the ancient Roman, but in fact—when the mask is whipped from his raw face—he turns out to be an abject hero, with the incriminating grin of the abject hero. The great blasphemy of Timothy McVeigh and Charles Manson is imposture, for they only pretend the gladiatorial collusion with the god, the *munus sine missione*. They are the abject gladiator, the hero who blames his mother.

"What was it," asks Carlin A. Barton in *The Sorrows of the Ancient Romans: The Gladiator and the Monster* (1993), "that drew free men to discard community, status, dignity, and power to fight in the arena, in the space allotted to the ruined and condemned?"

They lived in a world distended and fragile, topsy-turvy, at the verge of apocalypse.

"One finds in Roman literature," she continues, "from Cicero on, a sense that the price exacted for political, social and economic status (indeed, for life) had become self-abasement and that honor and dishonor had become synonymous. The traditional testimonials of power, freedom, and pride began to signal *as well* powerlessness, enslavement, and humiliation."

To become a gladiator was to become empowered, to die with "an unconquered neck." That is what the ancient Romans did. But to become an abject gladiator is to humiliate the audience as well as oneself.

As the licensed fool evolves into the Abject Hero of modern fiction, and then suffers the fusion of his abjection with *ressentiment,* the saturnalian dialogue turns into a grim trap in which the characters and the readers are equally caught. Undeniably, there is often a distinctly repellent quality in the characteristic "family traits" linking . . . Abject Heroes . . . , and yet our encounters can yield some of the exhilaration of any genuine engagement with the most dubious side of our imaginative identifications. From the impertinent slave of Augustan Rome to the unrepentant Collaborator of Vichy France, [these] voices . . . remind us, with a mixture of malice, cunning, and rage, that for them the carnival was always marked by bitterness and that the licensed fool whose jests, so we comfort ourselves, contain no slander, may already have shed his clown's motley [or, inversely, donned his tattoo] and begun to rail in earnest. The ensuing Saturnalia will indeed inaugurate Bakhtin's "carnival without footlights," but it will be experienced as a communal catastrophe of devastating proportion. The carnivalesque marketplace depicted in modern literature will be far different from the idealized image of a boisterous medieval fair or even from the safe confines of Diderot's Café de la Régence. Instead, the reader will follow an itinerary through a continent in ruins, in which insane murderers and shell-shocked victims stagger from one bombed-out castle to another. The most fitting slogan for this apocalyptic carnival is Céline's outcry toward the end of *Rigodon*: "That's what man has come to with all his immense, ecumenical, superatomic progress: everybody's in the arena and not a single spectator is left in the stands."

—MICHAEL ANDRÉ BERNSTEIN, *BITTER CARNIVAL*

So some of the victims of our time pretend to gladiatorial status; others pierce themselves. Both are transgressors. Manson and his like write their transgressive obscenities on the bodies of others, shaming the world with their acts. Those who pierce themselves remind one of Frankenstein's monster with a bolt through his neck, but with a significant difference: Those who pierce display themselves to the world with a bravery, a flare of *sprezzatura,* that the Frankenstein creature can only long to imitate, a gallantry of self-display that the Manson creature would spit at in fear. Piercing and other ways to inscribe messages upon one's own body are badges of chivalry. They mark a chivalrous confrontation with the goth darkness of the world, with the Waste Land T. S. Eliot described in 1921, "the dry stone" where "fear in a handful of dust" shakes the soul of man into an incoherence beyond the powers of God or the king's men or the esthetic austerities of modernism ever to put together again. "These fragments," Eliot says, in what might be a slogan for piercers, "I have shored against my ruins."

Piercers also give the finger to the owners of the world, who have done so well out of the world, and who now are beginning to pull up the NIMBY drawbridges to keep their first editions of *The Waste Land* (worth up to $3,000 in today's retro market) safe. It is time for a few words, then, about boomers, a generation for whom the gated community might have been specifically invented. It would be better, clearly, just to quote the whole of *Doonesbury,* a cartoon strip deeply and religiously and scathingly devoted to the examination of the boomer generations in America: the vast mass of self-conscious, belated, dysfunctional, busy, rise-obsessed men and women who now run the world, which they fill very full, and from which nowadays, now that they are no longer thirty-somethings, many of them, like Seinfeld, want to be safe.

Boomers, so populous and busy and articulate and caring (when they do not happen to be populous and busy and articulate and anti-caring), entered a world that seemed to be filling up with kith and kin; they are the first generation in the affluent West to feel acutely the rat-in-a-cage pressure of having to coexist with too many peers. For those of us who were lucky enough to have been born earlier into a slightly emptier world, and for those now in their twenties learning to be streetwise in a world their parents have already ransacked for meaning and bought the best plots in, the boomer generation bulks very large indeed. Their surges of mood affect us. Their increasing

Humanity must perforce prey on itself

Like monsters of the deep.

—WILLIAM SHAKESPEARE, *KING LEAR*

attentiveness to questions of aging in the populations of the affluent West are an ambiguous comfort to those of us old enough by now to know that gerontology is nothing more than an intense study of the last few inches of the plank. But boomers—at least those who grew up in the States and learned how to grasp lebensraum from the weak and to call it entitlement—do not, in their hearts, seem to think it *fair* that they too are walking the plank. That death is the end.

It may be the case that the apocalyptic anxieties so constantly adumbrated and explained in all the media of the Western world dominate our minds precisely because they represent the boomer generation's failure to come to terms with mortality, that the current fad for millennium fodder is a conversion hysteria of the billion boomers.

A *Guardian* report dated 12 May 1999 tells us that when the Disability Adjusted Life Year, or DALY (a criterion used by officials of the World Health Organization to measure the real cost of anxiety and depression worldwide) was applied to the affluent West, it was found that "neuropsychiatric conditions—from depression to alcohol or drug dependence, dementia and panic disorder—accounted for 23% of the disease burden, heart disease 18% and cancers 15%."

We have seen during the late 1980s and early adult men. It may have been associated with p

—DAVID NABARRO, WORLD HEALTH ORGANIZATION

These figures from the World Health Organization focus on the period when boomers determined the outcome of every survey taken in the affluent West, partly, of course, because there are so *many* of them. But it is also a consequence of the fact (which may be less a fact than a consensus of perception) that boomers have always needed to shift moods in coordination with one another. To move alone is to make the centipede stumble.

Because boomers don't break step on the bridge.

It could be argued, in contradistinction, that many older men and women, born early enough in the century to feel dissimilar to their peers, tend to come to their splendors and miseries by less predictable routes than have the boomers, who sometimes seem (from outside) very much like predatory fish in a feeding frenzy—though what they tend to eat is each other, themselves. It does seem, at times, that the boomers are the "lonely crowd" predicted by Vance Packard in the 1950s, that the accidie, the loneliness, the Waste Land torpor of the world is a boomer landscape.

990s a massive increase in the mortality of
ple's perceptions of the future.

So the world-historical shock of a mass conversion of boomers to millennial anxieties *could in itself* create the formal requirements for the realization of these anxieties.

The millennium is a midlife crisis for boomers.

Tragically, we are all caught in their dream.

In *Strange Things: The Malevolent North in Canadian Literature* (1995), Margaret Atwood examines in some depth a 1973 novel by the late Wayland Drew. *The Wabeno Feast* deals with two mythological creatures or visions: the Wendigo and the Wabeno. The former is the famous Native American creature, a tall, hissing demon with froglike eyes, always on the search for strangers. More important to us is the Wabeno, "a sorcerer of immense power." The protagonist, whose name is MacKay, witnesses a final coming together of these sorcerers, as Atwood paraphrases it:

These Wabenos are taller than usual and whiter than usual, owing to the fact that they have burnt their skins repeatedly by dancing in fire. This same activity has seared off their vital parts, and the watching MacKay comments, "I supposed I beheld a dream, a nightmare wherein fiends of neither sex made their mockery of both." The Wabenos are also cannibals, and the food at the "Wabeno Feast" of the title consists of one of their own members. The feast itself concludes with the whole island in flames.

It is not difficult to think of these Wabenos as figures of symbol. They are like Prospero, as played by Walter Pidgeon in *Fantastic Planet,* which we have already spoken about. The Wabeno, in other words, is one of the characteristic late-century images that we find in our own mirrors as we frantically dodge the issue: the fact that we and the island will burn in the same flame. That if we continue to deny our natures, deny our planet, deny our guilt, deny the potentials of our joy, then we will see in the mirror—as we awaken at the dawn of the millennium whose fires we have set ourselves, and which burn the world that is our only home—the white face of a castrato, contorted in anguish but refusing to look down at its seared member; in its jaws a human limb; in its hand a lit match.

For our consuming power over the world is in fact self-consumption. The people of the end times devour themselves, gloating all the while that they are doing no more than consuming what they have purchased, what they *own,* what they *deserve.*

We are the Wabeno Feast,
each and every one.
In the end, the whole island is in flames.

GUESSING RIGHT

Living as we do in the closing year of the twentieth century, enjoying the blessings of a social order at once so simple and logical that it seems but the triumph of common sense, it is, no doubt, difficult for those whose studies have not been largely historical to realize that the present organization of society is, in its completeness, less than a century old. No historical fact is, however, better established than that till nearly the end of the nineteenth century it was the general belief that the ancient industrial system, with all its shocking social consequences, was destined to last, with possibly a little patching, to the end of time.

—EDWARD BELLAMY, *LOOKING BACKWARD: 2000–1887*

At random, we glance at a file of *New York Times Book Review* sections. We land upon the issue for 12 January 1997. It is not a special issue; it does not stand out in any way. We look at the books being reviewed. Fully half of them, in one way or another, deal with the devastations human beings have lived through in the twentieth century, devastations both experienced or inflicted or both. Fully half of them are books that, indirectly, evoke thoughts of end times.

There are reviews of *The Idea of Biodiversity: Philosophies of Paradise,* by David Takacs; of *Fragments: Memories of a Wartime Childhood,* by Binjamin Wilkomirski; of *The Spears of Twilight: Life and Death in the Amazon Jungle,* by Philippa Descola; of *Impure Science: AIDS, Activism, and the Politics of Knowledge,* by Steven Epstein; of *Aftermath: The Remnants of War,* by Donovan Webster; of *Heaven and Earth: The Last Farmers of the North Fork,* by Steve Wick. None of these books is *about* the millennium, about a prefigured end of the world as such. They are not composed as attempts to self-fulfill numerological "prophecies." But every single one of them can be understood in terms of

It *was* the spirit world.
Vietnam.
Ghosts and graveyards.

I arrived in-country . . . in 1969, and walked . . .
in and around Pinkville,
through the villages of Thuan Yen
and My Khe and Co Luy.
I know what happened that day.
I know how it happened.
I know why. It was the sunlight.

It was the wickedness that soaks into your blood and slowly heats up and begins to boil. Frustration, partly. Rage, partly. The enemy was invisible. They were ghosts. They killed us with land mines and booby traps; they disappeared into the night, or into tunnels, or into the deep misted-over paddies and bamboo and elephant grass. But it went beyond that. Something more mysterious. The smell of incense, maybe. The unknown, the unknowable. The blank faces. The overwhelming otherness. This is not to justify what occurred on March 16, 1968, for in my view such justifications are both futile and outrageous. Rather, it's to bear witness to the mystery of evil. Twenty-five years ago, as a terrified young PFC, I too could taste the sunlight. I could smell the sin. I could feel the butchery sizzling like grease just under my eyeballs.

—TIM O'BRIEN, *IN THE LAKE OF THE WOODS*

We live, after all, in the aftermath of the

modernist project.

—ADRIAN SEARLE

the crisis we in the Western world know that we are facing, and which so many of us assume—consciously or unconsciously—has something to do with, or is somehow likely to climax at, the end of the century.

There is an animus in this book, but it is not against texts of this sort, for there is almost always an apocalyptic undertext in nonfiction written at the end of this century. Any animus here is against texts that wrap in cotton wool the apocalyptic undertext in terms of the millennium.

In London, a few days later in the same month, I was phoned by a colleague on the *Independent,* one of the quality British papers. He had a question. He'd just received the results of a poll taken by the famous Waterstone chain of bookstores, in which customers were asked what they thought were the five best novels of the twentieth century. The winner, by a huge margin, was J. R. R. Tolkien's *The Lord of the Rings* (1954–1955). My colleague wanted to know if I, as a critic of the literature of the fantastic, had any idea why this book might be so vastly popular. I told him what I thought.

The central lesson of the popularity of Tolkien, I suggested, lay in its confirmation of the power of story. Like all full fantasies written in the twentieth century, *The Lord of the Rings* reaffirmed our human need for stories to make sense of things. The austere accomplishments of modernism—the great works of T. S. Eliot, James Joyce, and others of their generation—may (or may not) represent pinnacles of art that Tolkien's looser and baggier vision cannot attain. But what they *did* demonstrate was that their success in repudiating the down-marketing of art and life throughout this century was also a failure, because the despair that infuses modernism (and make no mistake, modernist writers are profoundly, and perhaps rightly, despairing) did not enable those who read its texts with even the aesthetic semblance (or make-believe version) of a way out of this mess.

It is arguable that this despair—expressed in terms of a profound pessimism about modern life and the instruments that modern humans used to spiel that life—was the occasion of the famous modernist despite of story, which they replaced with artifacts of frozen telling, the vast array of self-referential devices, including the flashback, the frame within the frame within the frame behind another frame that isn't really there, and the epiphanic moment that burns through any semblance of a singular self being told in order to give us a timelessness of heaven (which is the opposite of story).

Tolkien, who began writing *The Lord of the Rings* during World War I, worked otherwise. His masterwork is a conscious countermyth to the twentieth century. He thought that "progress," technology, science, social relations, and even the failure of deference had all fabricated a profoundly inhumane world, a world teetering on the edge of moral and physical disaster. Despite advances in medicine and other spin-offs of science, the twentieth century was a place that Tolkien, fully consistent with the subversive subtext of all serious fantasy since the form took shape around the end of the eighteenth century, thought no sane person could ever choose to inhabit. The twentieth century, he thought, was simply *wrong*. *The Lord of the Rings* is an attempt to present not a vision in "realistic" terms of the precise kind of social world that we could imagine living in, but a countervision of humane life.

It is a vision in which the end times have been dodged, written by a man who thought we were in the midst of the end times.

A real life, Tolkien implies, cannot be led in the real twentieth century. Story makes meaning, and *The Lord of the Rings* claims that all true significance is story-shaped; but in the real twentieth century, Tolkien wishes to tell us, meaning has been eaten away, and we are lost in the dark, godless, bereft, estranged from our souls and our being. It is surely clear that as the century begins to end, human beings, especially those who live in the radically "modernized" Western world, do increasingly long for meaning.

The anxiety aroused by loss of story is a kind of pheromone of apocalypse. When human beings get a whiff of this pheromone, there is a instinctive response—one that may have had some adaptive significance over the many thousands of years of our tenancy of this world's soil—to displace.

Let's git the hell outta displace.

But there is nowhere to go. The Four Horsemen of our dreams bring, as it were, true plagues.

Overpopulation, degradation of the planet, nuclear war, the malnutrition of hundreds of millions of human beings at one time—all these plagues and more have become constants in our mind. We normalize the perils of the world, a ferociously powerful process. We are inside pollution, inside environmental degradation, just as we are inside the interstate system, just as we are inside Disneyland.

Death on a Pale Horse, Joseph Mallord/William Turner

For the world, which is too much to bear raw, interpenetrates us.

Definitions

Normalization: Any system normalizes any failure of any part of that system until it is too late.

The belly of the beast: From within, any system will appear to function as normal until it is too late.

Any system—any network of objects or focal points or human beings connected together by webs of information, neuronal similitude, distributed network, cross-references, tags, color codings, kin groups, family understandings, doppelganger *Umwelt* matrix pies, whatever—is a state of information. Information has two ingredients: reiteration (or memory) and novelty (what memory has to cope with). As a system ages, reiteration self-corrupts, and the new becomes unsortable. The millennium virus thrives in cultural systems whose reiteration components (religion, politics, family values) cannot cope with the new: evolution, global warming, overpopulation, the A-bomb, the end of the Cold War, the disintegration of the nuclear family (which never existed in the first place), the loss of deference, the loss of continuity, the anxieties of influence of an ancient culture (ours) too stiff and byzantine to bend the knee to tomorrow. But we human beings, caught in the chinks of the increasingly dysfunctional world machine, normalize our perceptions of things, so that the world machine continues to seem to function as normal until it's too late.

And anything that cannot be normalized, such as Charles Manson and those who have inherited his obscene abjectness of mien, is displaced.

The point at which a system is finally perceived to fall apart—during the still moment of Waste Land in the soul of its inhabitants—is *exactly* the point in a classic story that Aristotle calls the moment of recognition, when those who are living through a great tale begin to understand (or think they begin to understand) its true nature, and begin to move toward the climax, whether it be tragic or happy.

The lure of the millennium story is that it takes hold just as things are perceived to be genuinely collapsing. So that now, in the breathless hush of the Waste Land moment, it may be the case that we human beings on this planet will feel impelled to act out a drama that makes sense, that serves as a recognition of the stress and tumult and chaos and disintegration of the end times of this terrible century.

That moment of hush, when the angels at the four corners of the world hold their breath, may be the biggest toggle of all.

Definition

Toggle: A switch between before and after in the world, when a difference in degree turns visibly into a difference in kind. A toggle occurs when things not only change but *are seen to change*.

Examples of the toggle—though the term itself is not used—proliferate in the *State of the World* volumes issued annually by W. W. Norton on behalf of the Worldwatch Institute. Each volume, however full of reports of disaster avoidable and unavoidable, is constructed around the notion that it is still possible to make progress toward sustainable society. The authors of these volumes—Lester R. Brown, Christopher Flavin, Hilary French, and others, who were responsible for the 1999 volume, are typical—do, it must be admitted, convey an increasingly grim sense of things.

The idea of a toggle reflects a sense that it might be useful to concentrate our attention on *reversals of field* rather than on intensifications of symptoms through various spectrums, both in volumes such as *State of the World* and in our observation of life in general. A reversal of field occurs at that point in any graph of intensification when all that has happened becomes *before,* because the frame of reference has suddenly changed: either because we are able to see what is actually happening (that is, the system that blinded us, because we were within it, has finally, almost certainly too late, given us a perspective on the failure of the world machine), or because something new does actually happen at approximately the same time we notice it (though this is rare).

Toggles are centrally important in any attempt to understand that what is happening to the world is *new*. They are essential if we are to argue our way out of the fetish maze of the millennium into a present-tense awareness of apocalypse now. We must be able to recognize the light at the end of the tunnel. In this context, a toggle governs Robert Lowell's perception, in a famous couplet in "Day by Day," of the light switching into something else: "If we see the light at the end of the tunnel, / It's the light of the oncoming train." Toggles are significant parts of the grammar of the story of the world we are coming into.

Some toggles:

1. The point at which an increase in the efficiency of a technology no longer increases yield but actually *decreases* it—as in the fishing industry, which has used new technologies to scour many of its traditionally rich fisheries, such as the Grand Banks, into salt deserts.

2. The point at which the annual increase of irrigated land per person (an increase that has occurred throughout world history) becomes an annual decrease of irrigated land per person. This point was reached around 1985.

3. The point at which a great river first fails to reach the sea. Aspiring rivers include the Colorado, the Yellow, the Nile, and the Ganges.

4. The point at which fertilizer use, once governed by the prosperity of the country in question, is now governed by water availability.

5. The first year in the United States that the grain harvest does not meet consumption. The year was 1988.

6. Cropland was once expendable, and priced and valued and treated by governments accordingly (as it still is treated today in some regions). There is a point—it is the toggle point—when cropland is no longer expendable.

7. The ice cap that covers Greenland is melting slowly at the end of the century. As it does so, fresh water feeds into the heavily saline North Atlantic, gradually diluting its salinity. The effect of this is to reduce the interactive dynamic of the North Atlantic currents, including the Gulf Stream, with the very good chance that the Gulf Stream will flip-flop into quiescence and, consequently, northern European countries—including Great Britain and Norway—will experience a sudden harshening of their winters because of global warming. That flip-flop constitutes a toggle.

8. The date at which the last territory sacred to an indigenous tribe becomes a game preserve to which all unqualified persons are refused admittance.

9. The point at which, by standards of nutrition universally recognized, more people suffer malnutrition than the total population of the planet two hundred years ago, when Malthus first warned us about an inevitable race between folk and food.

10. The point at which, by standards of nutrition universally recognized, the number of obese people exceeds the number of those who are starving. In the United States in 1999, the number of obese men and women is pushing a hundred million.

11. The point at which, by standards of nutrition universally recognized, the number of starving people exceeds the number of those who are obese.

12. The point at which, on a worldwide basis, per capita production of grain begins to fall. Estimates vary, but there is some consensus that, in 1999, this particular toggle has switched.

13. The point at which the annual income of the billion poorest inhabitants of the planet falls below the asset value, measured in dollars, of the richest two men on the planet.

14. The point at which the annual income of the billion poorest inhabitants of the planet falls below the asset value, measured in dollars, of the richest man on the planet.

15. The point at which the amount of land given over to grain products begins to decrease, partly through urbanization, partly through degradation of cultivable land until it is no longer capable of growing crops. This point was reached in 1981.

The most important thing to keep in mind about the toggle is that it represents a shift in the intensity of meaning of that which is being affected. The man who is toggled into becoming a serial killer has somehow *guessed right*; he has entered suddenly into a life full of meaning. The river that no longer reaches the sea conveys to most hearts a sense of wrongness that is nothing if not meaningful. In a sense, toggling seems to save energy; it seems negentropic. But entropy is never defeated in the end, just displaced. The toggle events that make sense of lives or ecologies always cost the earth.

III

SO?

Malaria! said Tweedledum. Apocalypse! said Tweedledee. Malaria!! Apocalypse!!
—THE LITTLE BOOK OF APHORISMS OF THE END

Yep, son, we have met the enemy and he is us.

—WALT KELLY, POGO

But it will not avail to us to gaze upon the results of the dreams of the driven or the mad, or to desperately try to normalize out of consciousness the toggles that tell us something new is coming down the line. We cannot remain addicts of comfort-blanket paranoia shows such as the redoubtable *X-Files,* in the "lush, becalmed spirit of voyeurism so pure and intent that it borders on a trance state"—a state of passive fatalism that critics such as James Wolcott, quoted here, claim to see throughout America and the media-saturated affluent West.

For the people of the West, lassitude and horror combine in one gaze. Knowing that something is coming down the line, we stare at our television screens or our monitors as though the stories told there—*The X-Files* or *Millennium,* or the mazes of cyberspace we adhere to as though they were labyrinths we had only to pierce in order to reach final nirvana—could absolve us from reality. The story of the millennium, which is perhaps the most dangerous of these stories, as it absolves us from the whole of the world to come, must be abandoned.

It is 1999. We are at a crossroads. Hermes awaits us.

Come follow us, and smile as we;

> **We sail to the rock in the ancient waves,**

Where the snow falls by thousands into the sea,

> **And the drowned and the shipwrecked have happy graves.**

—THOMAS LOVELL BEDDOES, "SIBYLLA'S DIRGE"

The Sea of Faith
Was once, too, at the full, and round earth's shore
Lay like the folds of a bright girdle furled.
But now I only hear
Its melancholy, long, withdrawing roar,
Retreating, to the breath
Of the night-wind, down the vast edges drear
And naked shingles of the world.

Ah, love, let us be true
To one another! for the world, which seems
To lie before us like a land of dreams,
So various, so beautiful, so new,
Hath really neither joy, nor love, nor light,
Nor certitude, nor peace, nor help for pain;
And we are here as on a darkling plain
Swept with confused alarms of struggle and flight,
Where ignorant armies clash by night.

—MATTHEW ARNOLD, "DOVER BEACH"

HOW ARE Part Four TRICKS?

I lay in my bed in my house at dingy Hammersmith thinking about it all; and trying to consider if I was over- whelmed with despair at finding I had been dreaming a dream. . . .

All along, though those friends were so real to me, I had been feeling as if I had no business amongst them; as though the time would come when they would reject me, and say, as Ellen's last mournful look seemed to say,"No, it will not do; you cannot be of us; you belong so entirely to the unhappiness of the past that our happiness even would weary you. Go back again, now you have seen us, and your outward eyes have learned that in spite of all the infallible maxims of your day there is yet a time of rest in store for the world."

—WILLIAM MORRIS, *NEWS FROM NOWHERE*

GEEK GOOFS: Y2K

The first thing you'll notice
these figures have in common
is, they're both underwater
but don't seem to know it.
Or we could say they've been sunk
so long the terror has grown
familiar.

—FRED PFEIL, "SECOND CLASS LECTURE, SENIOR LIFESAVING COURSE"

The most terrible thing about waking up in the first dawn of the millennium will be the headache. Unless crazies have managed to take the helm of government overnight, or Unabombers have united in a worldwide midnight massacre, the first dawn of the new millennium is mainly going to be marked by hangovers.

There is one other possibility, of course. If—being as sensible as it's possible to be when one is talking about nonsense—we treat the birth of the millennium as taking place somewhere between the end of 31 December 1999 and the beginning of 1 January 2000, then there is of course one numbers-driven problem we're going to have to face.

The Y2K perplex—that is, the confusing obtuseness of those computers that have not been designed to cope with the change in their internal dating systems from 99 to 00—is certainly real enough. Mature men and women of science and technic have plausibly expressed worry about what may happen when millions of circuits—all of them embedded millions of layers deep in the pile of electronic crap our geek rulers have created for us over the past thirty years or so—go haywire, or simply fuse. What is utterly clear at this writing (early 1999) is that nobody *knows* what's going to happen.

A single circuit could blow or balk and cause a disaster.

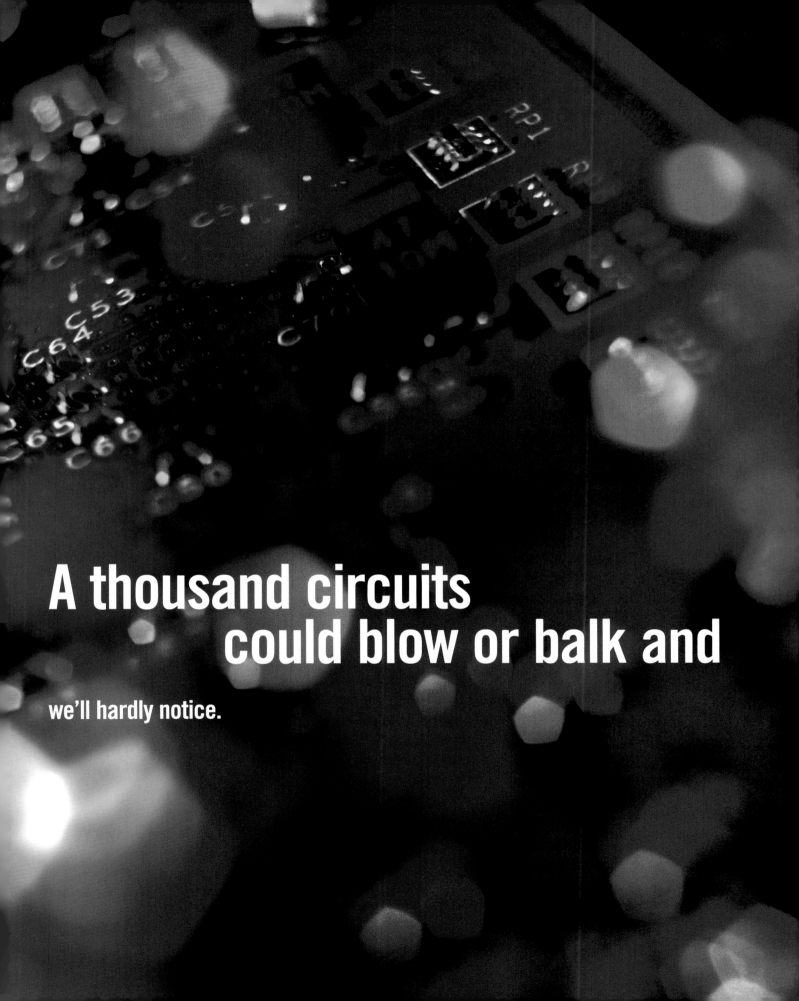

A thousand circuits
could blow or balk and

we'll hardly notice.

There is no way to know. There is no way to know how the almost infinitely intricate (but terribly stupidly constructed) electronic web we now live within actually works. We know the theory, but we haven't much more than a clue as to how—on the ground, buried deep within some power station, hidden behind used Kleenex in some air traffic controller's hellish kitchen, covered in concrete ten yards underneath the sewers that feed a world-famous hospital—the theory actually fits into the world. Indeed, if we did know exactly where what was, then we would have relatively little fear of midnight 1999–2000 exploding in our faces.

(A passing thought: Who the hell *were* these masked millionaires, these guys—almost certainly guys—who built into their computer designs the guarantee that they would suddenly turn inoperative at midnight 1999–2000? What were they thinking? We make fun of politicians and spin doctors, of social workers and other toilers in the terribly complex fields of human interactions, but their incompetence pales beside that of the geeks who turned their tinker's knowledge of computers—which are, after all, almost infinitely less complex than the dumbest juvenile delinquent—into nice little earners without a thought of the morrow. Did these guys not know there would be a year 2000? Did they not even begin to think about the implications of the fact that they had covered over the earliest generations of computer circuits with generation after generation of later additions? Did they think it didn't matter that they'd been creating new networks by piling new circuits on top of a literal midden of older and older circuits—which they forgot all about, and now found almost impossible to get back to? Did they think it didn't matter that—at least according to the most pessimistic of the experts now trying to fend off disaster—much of the modern computer-governed world, built as it is on unreachable archaic foundations, is going to fail because the circuits at the bottom of the midden were installed by geeks who never heard of the year 2000?)

Anything may happen.

Because the problem of Y2K is a problem in archeology.

Almost certainly, a good deal more is going to happen than some folk expect, and a great deal less than the pessimists hope. One of the dangers of warning against disaster—environmentalists are not immune to this—is a secret hope on the part of whistle-blowers for the disaster actually to occur, for them to be proven right after all. This understandable secret longing is particularly understandable when the warned-against disaster is long-term, slow in coming. Politicians do not respond well to expensive problems not due to ripen into disaster until after their terms of office are over. Whistle-blowers for Mother Earth—to which disasters happen more slowly than politicians are suited to detect—are treated as Cassandra was.

The secret behind the refusal to believe Cassandra is (1) that everything she says is obviously true, (2) that it is obviously the last thing anyone wants to hear, and (3) therefore it is the kind of utterance that conversion-hysteria systems are designed to avoid.

Newsweek

WHITE MALE PARANOIA

Are They the Newest Victims—or Just Bad Sports?

Come on then, cry'd Panurge, let's charge through and through all the Devils of Hell; we can but perish; and that's soon done. However, I thought to have reserv'd my Life for some mighty Battle. Move, move, move forwards. I am as stout as Hercules, my Breeches are full of Courage; my Heart trembles a little, I own, but that's only an effect of the coldness and dampness of this Vault; 'tis neither Fear nor an Ague: come on, move on, piss, pish, push on; my Name's William Dreadnought.

—RABELAIS, GARGANTUA AND PANTAGRUEL

What is most at risk when 2000 arrives and *some* systems at least will stub their toes will be the complex high-tech networks that have been built and rebuilt constantly, each new version like a further story added to an upside-down pyramid whose apex is stuck in the past and (literally) into the ground. The domino effects of glitches may well be felt throughout the various grids we nestle in—the power and telephone grids, the transportation networks. But precisely because any failures are likely to work in a domino fashion—one seizure in one primitive circuit buried in concrete somewhere triggering further seizures up the upside-down pyramid—it is impossible for us to predict the ultimate result. It is like playing chess—after only a few moves, the number of possible moves reaches toward the kind of numbers only supercomputers can crunch. But it is like playing chess with chessmen whose powers are not known, on a board whose number of squares changes by the millisecond, and according to only one fixed rule: Duck! You sucker.

I myself happen to travel fairly frequently by air. A year or so ago, I reminded myself to remember not to think about traveling during the night between 1999 and 2000. I am, in fact, surprised that airlines do intend to run flights at that time—just in case one of the dinosaurs sleeping at the bottom of the world traffic controller network does sneeze, dislodging a few trillion circuits before settling back down to sleep in the secure belief that the year 1900 had come again. Others of us who know that they do not know what is going to happen will do other things: stock up on drinking water, in case something clogs the works for a few precious days; stock up on preserves, in case the power goes; move into cash, in case the banks (against thousands of assurances that this will not happen—assurances I tend to believe) go walkabout, as they say in Australia, with our deposits.

So we have something to worry about. Or not. That must be rephrased, because that's millennial thinking. What we should say is that there are a whole number of things—all of which or some of which or none of which may actually happen—that we have to balance in our minds.

There is no one story out there.

There is nothing as abominably stupid as the millennium out there. No single tidal wave. No single explosion. No single anything. We have never lived in a world in which the millennium was possible—and now, in 1999, we no longer live in a world in which it is even *conceivable*.

Despite so many people's need for a simple story, there's too much happening out there for the millennium to cope with.

The seas are going to be too rough for the Revelation ark.

GEEK GOOFS: SCIENCE FICTION

It might be worth our while to step back for a moment from the terrible pass we have gotten ourselves into, as citizens of the world's longest-running numbers racket. As members of the Western world, we have been mouthing the lines of a single hit for hundreds of years now. Earlier in this book we saw what happens to the words of that hit—the story of a history of relentless rise, of unending victory for the kind of people who became us—when it no longer cuts ice. What happened was that—faced with the cross tides and turmoils of the last years of this century, where we all have to live, despite our Tamagotchi gestures toward a touchable past—the story of the rise of the Western world did not so much end as become mute.

That silence was not restricted to folk such as the editors of *Life*. Take, for instance, the genre of literature whose great subject was the twentieth century, whose secret strength was its readers' sense that the stories they read were manuals designed to teach all of us how to make the twentieth century actually *work*. Take, for instance, science fiction. It is the genre I myself have spent most of my adult years studying. I have loved it, in my fashion, for half a century; but when I look back at its accomplishments and failures from the coign of vantage of century's end, I find myself gripped by what must be called a sense of pathos. For science fiction was not only an aggressive dream of the future, but the dream (or illusion) that it could, through the powers of the proactive imagination of the wannabe secret masters who wrote and read it, actually shape that future. But now, in 1999, the worlds of science fiction—by which I mean both the worlds in which it was written and the worlds it dreamed might come—are irretrievably remote. They are worlds of *ago*, because the worlds of the dream of the future of science fiction became us.

Many dates have been suggested for the first science fiction novel, from the epic of Gilgamesh on down. This essentially twentieth-century genre can be seen as springing from utopian discourse—Sir Thomas More's *Utopia* (1516) is both the most famous example of the utopia and the book that gives the form its name—and inspiring the work of Aldous Huxley, George Orwell, and other famous "non-sf" writers of sf in the twentieth century. Or we can think of it as evolving from the fantastic voyage (there were dozens of them in classical literature, most now lost) and coming to flower in the works of Jules Verne and E. E. Smith. Or we can combine utopian discourse and the fantastic voyage, and breed from this mix the oddest and most private and most intensely combative form of twentieth-century sf, hard sf—stories ostensibly based on hard scientific speculations, but secretly more wild-eyed than any other form of the genre. Here is where writers such as Larry Niven and Gregory Benford and David Brin and Greg Bear clash like moderately ectomorphic dinosaurs in the mists of time forward.

Or we can think of sf as a corruption of the British scientific romance as written by H. G. Wells before the turn of the century and brought to complex maturity by Olaf Stapledon, Arthur C. Clarke, and Brian Aldiss. This is the kind of "science fiction" that—to Hollywood's taste, at least—pays all too little attention to what was, until recently, the big story of sf. The authors of the scientific romance did not, perhaps, expect Hollywood attention. With the exception of a couple of remote spin-offs from Wells's *The War of the Worlds* (1898), the only real media success for any scientific romance has been *2001: A Space Odyssey* (1968), the film Stanley Kubrick expanded out of a Clarke short story. And even that was—compared with the box-office takings of regressive children's stories such as *Star Wars*—a *succès d'estime*. After all, *2001* is a film about the profound depression of the human race at the cusp of the millennium. From the perspective of 1968, it suggests that by the year 2001 we will be so incapable of living in the new steel-beach worlds of near space—was there ever a more depressing lot of protagonists than the crew en route to the moon?—that we will need the arbitrary help of an alien artifact maybe billions of years old to skyhook us out of the doldrums. This is far too realistic an assessment of the demoralized, displaced, theme-park, retro behavior of humanity in 1999 to have come from an sf mentality.

Or we can think of sf as an evolution from the rationalized Gothics of writers such as Mary Shelley, whose *Frankenstein* (1818)—to the continued irritation of those who prefer to think of sf as wonderment sprung from the forehead of Hugo Gernsback in 1926—was taken by Brian Aldiss as the first sf novel of all. But of course Aldiss is not an American and has no loyalty to Gernsback's immigrant epiphanies about the future of the proud land he had settled in. He has no reason to think of this form of literature as being bound to the one story of America. We, however, do.

Thinking about sf as rationalized Gothic—while remembering at the same time that sf in the movies was until recently, for budget and bias reasons, *always* told in terms of horror—leads us into an apparent diversion. But it may help us understand a quite extraordinary thing about the most popular form of sf in 1999: the sf movie. I may be remembering selectively here, but maybe not. Here is the question: Has there been in the last twenty years one single sf movie that depicts the near future in positive terms?

Or does every sf movie that talks about the near future talk about it as something terrible?

We can put to one side the various exudates of the *Star Trek* stable, because the basic future depicted in that series was devised by Gene Roddenberry around 1965, and that basic future—which is little more than an enabling backdrop—reflects the vague liberal bias both of Roddenberry and of his era. One of the reasons *Star Trek* was not particularly popular in the 1960s was that its vision of the future failed to strike an original chord with its audience: It was just more of the chromium Futurama vista, complete with nuclear families in futuristic vehicles, that we were all familiar with then, and which we were already, in 1966–68, beginning to distrust.

Star Trek failed in the 1960s because it was old-fashioned, but not old-fashioned enough.

Star Trek only came into its own a few decades later, when the future it depicted had changed from a cliché to a counterfactual. Viewers became loyal to Captain Kirk and his Teletubby crew when they began to seem conspicuously retro, when they began to represent a vision of a future we knew we were never going to experience. (I personally always find myself thinking of *Star Trek* viewers as coming from the same disaffected cohort of men and women as those who buy vast gas-guzzling SUVs, most of which will never stray off a paved road into the fragments of wilderness left us. Like alien abductions, the SUV is a manifestation of conversion hysteria.) *Star Trek* takes us away from now, all right—but in exactly the wrong direction, just as *Babylon 5,* dressed in the sheep's clothing of a fashionable (but clean-cut) version of cyberpunk, takes us in the wrong direction: forward to the past.

So, putting *Star Trek* to one side, what remains on film of the big story of sf, the story of a progress from ignorance and bondage to earth into a better, bigger set of worlds to come?

The story for which the millennium was an open door?

What we actually see on our screens—what we go in our millions to see on our screens—is almost invariably a vision of disintegration and paralysis, as in *Blade Runner* (1982), the *Alien* movies, *Total Recall* (1990), or *Waterworld* (1995). Those governments that exist either are palpably corrupt or represent (as in *The Handmaid's Tale* [1990], which was based on Margaret Atwood's 1985 vision of dystopia) some form of fundamentalism gone sour. And if the future visits *us*—as in the *Terminator* movies, or *Millennium* (1989)—we can be certain that life up the line is far more dreadful than it is even now.

So. Science fiction movies are unanimous:
It's going to be awful up the line.

*"I shit in your albu

But that's not the true and final point. Certainly sf movies are as unlikely as sf fiction to depict the near future in positive terms. Whether we think of sf as evolved utopian discourse, or fantastic voyage, or scientific romance, or rationalized Gothic, what we do know is that no one writing in any version of any of these modes of sf is very cheerful about the near future. (It is a cliché of sf criticism that most sf writers, since about 1980, tend to set their novels as far beyond the near future as they dare, in order not to have to talk about the awfulness in store for us around the next corner.) What we also know, however, is that most sf writers, until very recently, have been as restricted in their visions as most filmmakers.

The one thing all the movies we've mentioned hold in common—over and above their unfailing pessimism—is that for each of them the future is one thing. In this they are, unfortunately, only following the lead of most sf writers, who until recently, at least in America, used the armamentarium of their genre to depict monocular futures. There are reasons for this.

For many years, sf writers wrote within (and shaped) a consensus about the future: It was (as we've already hinted) a version of the twentieth century that had been made to work, a twentieth century that cashed out. This vision, which

** said the Horseman.

infused the dreams of Americans from the first years of this century, became inextricably allied, in the minds of sf writers, with the appliances they selected to dramatize this triumph of tinkering: the rockets, the robots, the flying cities. All these exemplified a dream of realized efficacy, and by virtue of using them in stories, sf writers found themselves affirming values they did not necessarily approve of consciously, while at the same time creating futures that would work only if everything did in fact work out as planned: but nothing, in the real world, ever does.

The terrible drab secret of twentieth-century sf was that it was made of stories that had to work exactly.

If they didn't work exactly, they *broke*. No wiggle room.

The single-vision futures of sf were terribly fragile. The future of big-story sf, like the future of reactive scenarios that attempted to teach big corporations in the 1990s how to streamline their past so they could slip into the future without facing fundamental change, was a *niche* future.

This niche drabness of the future depicted by most sf until recently bears a humiliatingly close relationship to mil-lennial thought in general. Both techniques of envisioning are fixative techniques: They represent attempts to hold to the story. They are binary in nature—either the world described exists, or its opposite exists. There is never a sense that Robert A. Heinlein's "future history," which he devised in the early 1940s, could ever do more than flash a strobe light into a maze of possibilities; when Heinlein himself in the early 1960s began to realize that the future wasn't working, he retreated to a nihilistic solipsism, and his last novels—such as *The Number of the Beast* (1980) or *To Sail Beyond the Sunset* (1987)—contemptuously mocked the old certainties of sf by incorporating into their texture so many alternative universes that none made sense, none mattered.

In binary thinking there are no grays, no mutabilities, no muskegs of futurity whose nature will never be known, any more than we can know tomorrow's weather, except in general. Binary thinking, as we've been hinting through-out, is *anxious* thinking; it is hysterical thinking. The polymorphic perversity of Heinlein's last years is a sign of panic. At this point of despair, the imagination fixes to something or some story, perhaps not a very relevant or interesting vision, and refuses to let go—just as the dodo refused to let go of Mauritius.

We know that millennial thinking permeates the end times; this book has assumed throughout precisely that this is the case. We also know that scenario thinking (see below) has permeated the end times. We need also to under-stand that sf thinking—as it has promulgated itself through fashion and film and architecture, and through the phenomenon, new to history, of a population that at least claims to be ready for the next thing—has also perme-ated, until very recently, the end times.

No wonder we're in more trouble than the trouble we're in.

In the last quarter of the twentieth century, at a time when Western civilization was declining too rapidly for comfort and yet too slowly to be very exciting, much of the world sat at the edge of an increasingly expensive theater seat, waiting—with various combinations of dread, hope, and ennui—for something momentous to occur.
—TOM ROBBINS, *STILL LIFE WITH WOODPECKER*

We do know, after all, that it's going to be a very harsh few decades for the human race on this planet.

We know that the dreams of apocalypse we have are not foolish dreams: anything but. We know that we may not, in fact, come through. But we also know, or we should be beginning to guess, that the old stories—the Whig his-tory of progress; the millennium of the fundamentalists; the unilateral dark futures of sf books and movies; the gated-community America that most corporate scenarios end up, willy-nilly, planning to take advantage of—no longer work. They are, all of them, built on a linear understanding of the world that derives from the linear sacred dramas of both Christianity and Islam. It is an understanding that entails clear binary outcomes: we win or we lose; we are saved by the Rapture or we are damned; we escape the planet or die in a stink of pollution down here; we close the doors of our homes and hearts or we turn into members of the third world and starve to death growing for American agribusiness crops we cannot afford to purchase. This is the shape of our expectations: yes or no.

"So," he said. "You're what we'd call a survivalist? You think that when it all falls apart we should pack up and head for the hills?"

"No." Now she did sound offended. "Of course not. We're human beings. We got where we are by cooperating, by helping each other. It's just that the future is so dangerous."

"Yep."

"We're going to have to be smart to survive, on any timescale you care to think about. My dad says he thinks I went a little crazy, back when I was a kid. But I think I went a little sane. It was like waking up. It seems to me that everyone else is a little crazy, not me." She was looking out over the city, and the last of the sunlight picked out her profile, her strong nose and chin.

He said, "Maybe you're too sane. Nobody should be burdened with too much future."

—STEPHEN BAXTER, *MOONSEED*

And it's all wrong.

No one is going to say, in 1999, that it can't all go wrong in the next century. As we've already said, it might all go wrong crossing the infinitely tiny gap between 31 December 1999 and 1 January 2000, when all the circuits may crash (though it is most unlikely that they will, as it is most unlikely that the geeks who bungled the job of building our electronic environment for the last thirty years will have had the infernal efficiency to fuck everything up in one millisecond; no, that's very probably beyond them). It might, but it probably won't. What we'll probably face on the morning of 1 January 2000 is more of the same.

But more of the same is precisely what the millennium story is incapable of handling, what the big story of science fiction has failed to anticipate, what the scenario writers for huge corporations significantly miss.

More of the same is *us*.

It might be worth taking a further look at science fiction—because the big-story sf we've been talking about is a thing of the past.

Why is order so wonderful? Why must we praise it so? Why is it identifiable with all human value? Why do we see it when it is not even there? We have seen why: we praise order because it is an adaptational necessity for us that we experience order. And our praise merely reinforces the greatest of all human mottoes: *Millions for the orientation but not one cent for reality.*

—MORSE PECKHAM, *MAN'S RAGE FOR CHAOS: BIOLOGY, BEHAVIOR, AND THE ARTS*

This is not to deny that most sf written—or if that's not quite the case, most sf that's *published*—today is, reprehensibly, retro stuff: novelizations and realizations tied to series owned by massive proprietors (such as Paramount for *Star Trek* or Fox for *The X-Files* or *Millennium*) whose main concern is product control—whose main motive for getting captive writers to labor in the fields of sharecrop is that of selling books to addicts. Paramount and Fox (and Disney and several other massive corporations) are *owners*. If sf had a genome (rather than the kind of loose up-to-now-uncopyrightable structure I've been trying to articulate here), then these organizations would be vying to gain absolute copyright control over it.

That would be the great betrayal they can only aspire to at the moment.

Because it cannot be said too often: If the work of great literature is to threaten us with the new, to make us see the world afresh, then the function of the entertainment business today is to soothe us with the old, to praise us for our reluctance to look freshly at anything.

And when He broke the seventh seal, there was silence in heaven for half an hour.

—— REVELATION, 8:1

Novelizations and their ilk——which in 1999 make up a high percentage of many prestigious publishers' lists——are a kind of slow poison. They poison us to the new. It is yet another sign of the displacement activities of the anxious that so many "novels" are sold whose only function is to repeat stories that were poisonously false to the world to begin with. "Original" novels by the Danielle Steels of the world may also falsify reality according to strict criteria that demand that any novelty contained be consumed by elements that repeat safe lies already told. Novels of this sort——whether written for hire for the owners of our mass media, or "created" by more powerful authors who own their own copyright——poison our capacity to live in the next century.

Science fiction as a whole has only very reluctantly abandoned its fixated reiteration of the big story——the *Star Trek* story, as it were.

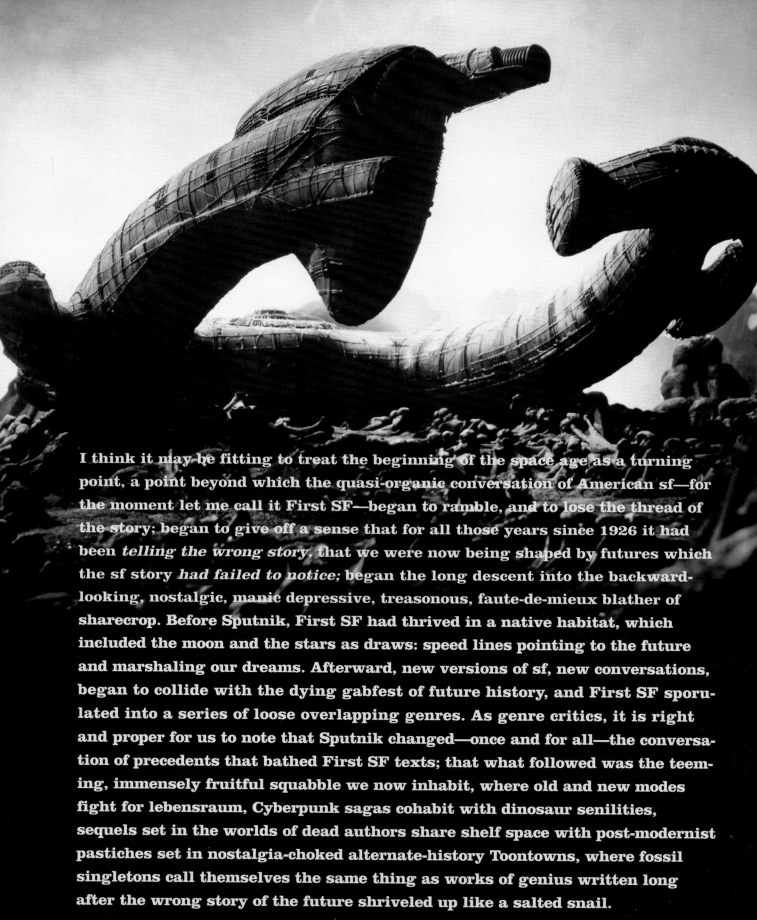

I think it may be fitting to treat the beginning of the space age as a turning point, a point beyond which the quasi-organic conversation of American sf—for the moment let me call it First SF—began to ramble, and to lose the thread of the story; began to give off a sense that for all those years since 1926 it had been *telling the wrong story*, that we were now being shaped by futures which the sf story *had failed to notice;* began the long descent into the backward-looking, nostalgic, manic depressive, treasonous, faute-de-mieux blather of sharecrop. Before Sputnik, First SF had thrived in a native habitat, which included the moon and the stars as draws: speed lines pointing to the future and marshaling our dreams. Afterward, new versions of sf, new conversations, began to collide with the dying gabfest of future history, and First SF sporulated into a series of loose overlapping genres. As genre critics, it is right and proper for us to note that Sputnik changed—once and for all—the conversation of precedents that bathed First SF texts; that what followed was the teeming, immensely fruitful squabble we now inhabit, where old and new modes fight for lebensraum, Cyberpunk sagas cohabit with dinosaur senilities, sequels set in the worlds of dead authors share shelf space with post-modernist pastiches set in nostalgia-choked alternate-history Toontowns, where fossil singletons call themselves the same thing as works of genius written long after the wrong story of the future shriveled up like a salted snail.

—JOHN CLUTE, "PILGRIM AWARD SPEECH"

It has only very slowly abandoned the twentieth century, only reluctantly turned its gaze on what seems likely to be the realities of the next. One of the reasons for this reluctance is, of course, the fact that media-minded publishers are less interested in stories about the new than they are in product lines, which by definition repeat the past.

Another reason is that it hurts.

This is the hurt of the new. That which we have not already become used to is almost certainly going to be painful—or at the very least a great deal of work—to understand. It is just as bad for writers as it is for anyone else. By about 1975 or 1980, science fiction had become a genre of the familiar. While soothing its readers and publishers and writers and exploiters with the tall story that it was addressing the thousand futures tumbling around our ears, it turned out in reality to be a security blanket.

Like millennialism.
        Like hysteria.

To obey the "rules" of the old science fiction was to engage in a Tamagotchi gesture of the imagination.
        Many of us did so.

Quite legitimately, the first edition of the *Encyclopedia of Science Fiction,* which was conceived in 1975 and designed to attempt to encompass the sf that had been written up to about that point, concentrated on big-story sf. The general editor of that edition, Peter Nicholls, devised the term "conceptual breakthrough"—that moment at which a new paradigm of perception or knowledge replaces, usually convulsively, the old—to describe the central movement of sf.

It wasn't our fault a quarter of a century ago that "conceptual breakthrough" would turn out to be a historical description: that it would turn out to describe First SF to a nicety, but singularly fail to describe the kind of sf now being written by live talents.

Over the last few decades, sf has begun to lose its profound attachment to the old set of Fables of the First World: tales whose protagonist, usually human, represents the dominant species in the venue being described, the species which knows how to get to the future. I think that sf stories today are more and more beginning to sound like Fables of the Third World: stories whose protagonists, often human, represent cultures which have been colonized by the future. The future may come in the form of aliens, or the catnip nirvana of cyberspace, or as AIs, or as bioengineered transformations of our own species: but whatever it touches, it subverts. Sf stories of this sort can—depressingly—read rather like manuals designed to train Polynesians in the art of begging for Cargo; but they can also generate a sense of celebration of the worlds beyond worlds beyond our species' narrow path.

—JOHN CLUTE, "PILGRIM AWARD SPEECH"

What we are facing now is not the millennium, which is one future, but the year 2000, which is a dozen—a hundred—futures all jostling for room on this one planet. The sf that is being written now about the next five to fifty years is sf about *surfing*. It is sf about the kind of people it will take to cope with a hundred futures rather than one, and it will be about the kind of societies they will fabricate and inhabit.

It is when we look at a novel such as Bruce Sterling's *Distraction* (1998), set forty years down the line, at a time when a thousand things are happening at once (just as they are now), that we begin to understand how it may be possible to establish models for understanding—even if we no longer *rule*—the worlds we are increasingly inhabiting.

In Sterling's year 2040 or so, the United States of America has become fractal: no universally honored central government survives,

Bambakias swallowed painfully and raised one bony finge[r] govern with a political culture that fragmented. And the parti[es] education system has collapsed. Our health system is so ba[d] We're in a State of Emergency.

"You're not telling me anything new here," Oscar chided. [He] bowl. "Are you going to finish that?"
—BRUCE STERLING, *DISTRACTION*

so that the more familiar one is with any region or settlement of like-minded men and women, the more complex it all becomes, the more each individual facet of the world resembles an entire world of polity and adherence, heresy and ritual and iconicity and secret journeys to the core. Those who survive in this environment have themselves become more tribal, thinking of themselves in terms of almost immeasurably complex networks of local and—through the information web—universal loyalty and touch.

Although Sterling clearly does not wish to prognosticate any sort of outcome to this period of profound mobility—indeed, he is very careful *not* to call it an interregnum between the relatively fixed world of the twentieth century and some new fixity up the line—it is also clear he's fully aware of the resemblance between his imagined near future and the chaos and incoherence (for instance) that marked the slow end of the Roman Empire, the slow rappelling downward to the Dark Ages of civilized men and women making do, as best they could, with the junk and jewels of the past.

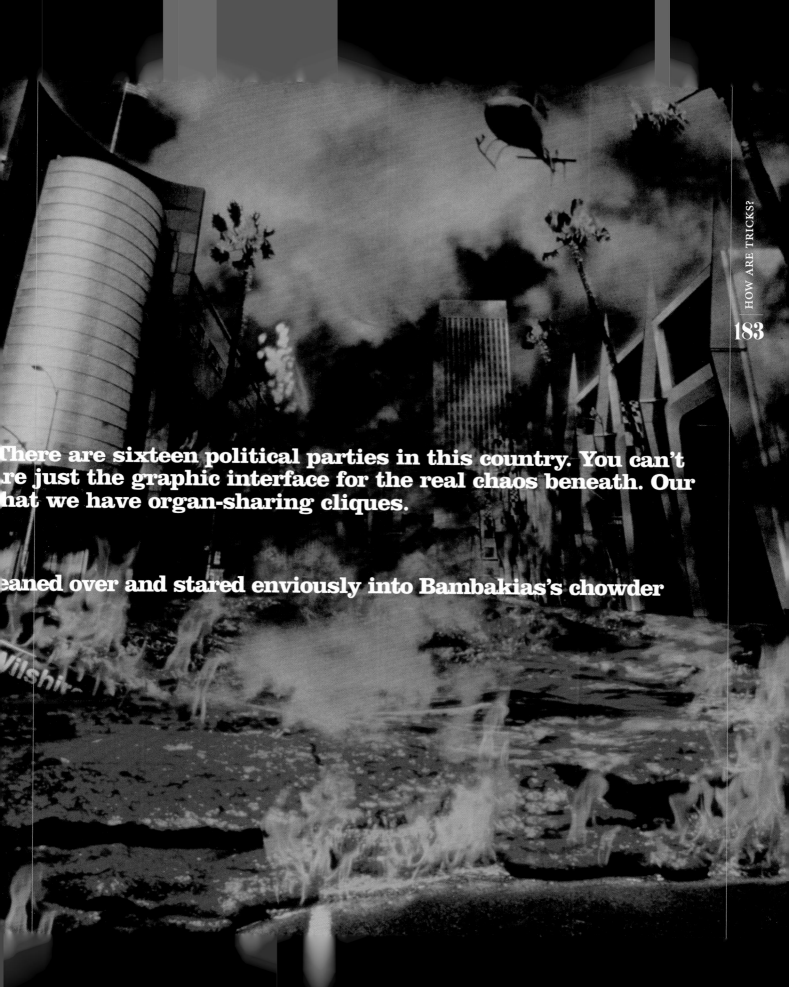

There are sixteen political parties in this country. You can't re just the graphic interface for the real chaos beneath. Our hat we have organ-sharing cliques.

eaned over and stared enviously into Bambakias's chowder

Oscar, the protagonist of the book, is what in 1999 we would call a spin doctor; but half a century on, spin doctoring is no longer the morally repugnant manipulation of otherwise stable truths that we deem it (pretty naively) to be today. In 2040 a spin doctor is a surfer of the riptides of information; he (in this case it's a he) stays upright like a buoy in those tides, balancing himself in a world—a thousand worlds—made up of intersections, fumblings, understandings and misunderstandings, dealings, sellings, and tradings: boundaries. Like the spy boy who performs his dance on the magical boundary between audience and actors in the Mardi Gras parade, like Hermes, he mediates the crossroads.

In a world where information gluts the senses and spam jams sleaze over the World Wide Web, Oscar is the true hero. His biceps are minuscule, but he spins the glut. He treats his clients as functionally identical with the proactive image of themselves he creates for them—an image that can be understood topologically as a critical-pathing of the route humans need to follow in order to survive and succeed in the new age—so that his customers are no longer passengers in a ship drifting through alien seas, but the ship itself.

Oscar is the kind of human being we need to become.

The last thing in the world Oscar would ever countenance for himself, or for one of his clients, would be getting stuck in one story.

He believes in no God
—or, rather, he believes in a lot of them.

Oscar is a denizen of the border country, the water margins, where polytheism flourishes. He lives between versions of the world, and he rides them.

He is a trickster. He is what Case—the protagonist of William Gibson's brilliant *Neuromancer* (1984), a book that arguably did as much to create cyberspace as pre–World War II science fiction did to create the space race—cannot quite get free enough of his past to accomplish. When Case dives into cyberspace he acts like a big-game hunter in darkest Africa; when Oscar surfs the infinitudes of the Net circa 2040 he is in his element.

I think that life would suddenly seem wonderful to us if we were threatened to die as you say. Just think of how many projects, travels, love affairs, studies, it—our life—hides from us, made invisible by our laziness which, certain of a future, delays them incessantly.

But let all this threaten to become impossible for ever, how beautiful it would become again! Ah! if only the cataclysm doesn't happen this time, we won't miss visiting the new galleries of the Louvre, throwing ourselves at the feet of Miss X, making a trip to India.

The cataclysm doesn't happen, we don't do any of it, because we find ourselves back in the heart of ordinary life, where negligence deadens desire. And yet we shouldn't have needed the cataclysm to love life today. It would have been enough to think that we are humans, and that death may come this evening.

—MARCEL PROUST

THE MILLENNIUM SOFT-SHOE

The only picture on the walls was a framed reproduction of a Piero di Cosimo that's in the National Gallery—a satyr bending over a dead or dying nymph with a wound in her throat. They are on the shore of a bay. A sad brown dog watches the two of them. Other dogs play on the beach; there are herons and a pelican. In the blue distance ships ride at anchor; beyond them are the buildings of a port. The scene is magical, dreamlike, desolate; the nymph, covered only by a bit of drapery over her hips, her girlish breasts pathetically exposed, is so luminously beautiful—her death seems a dream-death. She and the satyr seem to have strayed into a dream of the death of innocence.

"Do you think they'll wake up?" I said.

Mr. Rinyo-Clacton turned away from the desk to look, first at the pictured, then at me. "They won't and you won't. This is it."

—RUSSELL HOBAN, *MR. RINYO-CLACTON'S OFFER*

Tricksters may still be scarce on the ground—or hardly recognized when they butt themselves into our lives—but there are, all the same, thousands of ways to behave available to us in 1999, in which year the Hopi "messenger" Thomas Banyacya died at the age of eighty-nine, just a few years after he had sprinkled cornmeal on the podium in front of the United Nations General Assembly and told those few delegates present that world leaders must begin to listen to the harmony of the earth.

The 15,000 or so Hopis are a small nation, but their sense of burden is great. According to a 900-year-old religious tradition, the Great Spirit Maasau'u, Guardian of the Earth, assigned them the duty of preserving the natural balance of the world and entrusted them with a series of ominous prophecies . . . [which] remained a secret oral tradition until 1948, when Hopi religious leaders, alarmed by reports of the atomic bomb's mushroom cloud, which they saw as the destructive "gourd of ashes" foretold in the prophecies, appointed Thomas Banyacya and three others as messengers to reveal and interpret the prophecies to the outside world. . . .

A fierce opponent of uranium mining and a variety of other industrial assaults on the environment, Mr. Banyacya warned that an endless quest for material wealth would destroy the balance of the world; yet he did not reject all modern conveniences. His United Nations address and several other messages can be found on the Internet at www.alphacdc.com/banyacya/banyacya.html, a site maintained by the Alpha Institute.

—ROBERT MCG. THOMAS JR., OBITUARY OF THOMAS BANYACYA IN THE *NEW YORK TIMES*

There are available to us, almost on demand, thousands of planned presentations of self in everyday life. We have very many more ways to behave than our grandparents ever dreamed of. I first wrote these words in the midcoast region of the American state of Maine, and later revised them in Camden Town, a recently fashionable area fairly close to the center of London, England.

In Maine I encountered men and women whose lives have not visibly changed since the hardscrabble days of (say) 1950; all their lives they have coped with the kind of change the vast majority of men and women have had to cope with since agriculture began. The change they cope with is *hardship*.

Not enough work. The rotting of the land. The loss of wildlife to shoot. Death. Taxes. But that's changing. Now the kind of change they mostly encounter—now, in 1999, that money from Away is pouring selectively into their old homeland—is the sort of change middle-class folk find seductive but confusing because it presents itself in terms of amelioration. New roads. Lots of new houses to share the tax burden. Convenience stores. The vast addictive fluorescent aisles of Wal-Mart and Ames and Shaw, where the disappointments of American life are not contradicted but soothingly *confirmed* (it is, after all, hard to avoid the thought that American culture in general is constructed around rituals of disappointment management). The old-timers of Maine flock to Wal-Mart in order to alleviate the sense that they are alone in their disappointment, alone in the inevitable failure of their attempts to manage hardship and mortality.

Life is a process of breaking down and using other matter, and if need be, other life. Therefore, life is aggression, and successful life is successful aggression. Life is the scum of matter, and people are the scum of life. There is nothing but matter, forces, space and time, which together make power. Nothing matters, except what matters to you. Might makes right, and power makes freedom. You are free to do whatever is in your power, and if you want to survive and thrive you had better do whatever is in your interests. If your interests conflict with those of others, let the others pit their

The mass of men lead lives of quiet desperation.

—HENRY DAVID THOREAU

power against yours, everyone for theirselves. If your interests coincide with those of others, let them work together with you, and against the rest. We are what we eat, and we eat *everything*.

All that you really value, and the goodness and truth and beauty of life, have their roots in this apparently barren soil.

This is true knowledge.
--KEN MACLEOD, *THE CASSINI DIVISION*

Their view of the millennium—those who bother to think about it—is a kind of bone-weary binarism: It may mean the end, or it may mean zilch. The old-timers of Maine, who were always victims of economic and corporate forces beyond their control, continue to think of themselves as bound to the wheel of America Away; it may be that in this they prefigure the abject lassitude of most other Americans and most everyone elsewhere as they face the new century, as they pop the millennium pill with its addictive message that it all makes sense. It doesn't, of course. When we look too closely at the new world, what we see, in fact, is chaos.

Chaos does not forgive.
The new century will not forgive our addiction to the millennium pill.

In Maine it is possible, too, to see what the newcomers do in order to stave off the end. Many of them have spent most of their adult lives—since emigrating there—within five or ten miles of the coast. Old hippies, old lawyers, old artists: They inhabit Maine as though it were a tidal backwater, with niches galore for archaic species to colonize, in order to stave off the terrors of change. The niche species of *Homo sapiens* who inhabit Maine—and who closely resemble the niche species of *Homo sapiens* who inhabit the western slope of Colorado, and who bask under the mountains of the Pacific Rim—are like living scenarios. They have scenarioed their lives and their environments to optimize their chances of living out their natural spans. In the Western world, which is affluent enough to allow its inhabitants to think in terms of scenarios rather than simply praying to survive the night, there are millions of human beings whose lives are isomorphic with the scenario-driven strategy of any corporation hoping to ride out whatever turmoil lies in store.

The difference between a corporation in 1999 following niche scenarios by which they hope to survive the turmoil and Oscar morphing his way through waves of reality change is that corporation gurus today inwardly anticipate

Day of Victory, McKendree Robbins Long

Wind, jolly huntsman, your neat bugles shrilly,
Hounds make a lusty cry;
Spring up, you falconers, the partridges freely,
Then let your brave hawks fly.
Horses amain
Over ridge, over plain,
The dogs have the stag in chase.
'Tis a sport to content a king.
So, ho! ho! through the skies
How the proud bird flies,
And sousing, kills with a grace.
Now the deer falls; hark! how they ring.

—THOMAS DEKKER, *THE SUN'S DARLING*

that after they have ridden out the storm, the winds will subside and the old contours of reality will take shape through the dying mist of change. Oscar hopes to survive, but he never expects to return.

When they come to Maine—individuals of an artistic bent or retirees hoping to preserve false memories of the golden past or corporations looking for environmentally vulnerable cheap labor—they do what any espouser of a reactive scenario does to the world around him or it: They apply the anesthetic of preventive ownership to the land they have invaded. They novelize the world around them into a story that runs on ruts, in order to continue to own it. They buy into the old chaos of history and attempt to freeze it shut; they "defend" the traditional ways in the same way that Walt Disney defends mice. Just as their lives are shaped as reactive scenarios, so their environments are shaped after the model of the theme park, the ultimate story that runs on ruts. Every golf course—in Maine or anywhere—is a theme park of something that was once real; every golf course—over and above the human tragedies who actually play golf—is a denial of the breath of the world.

So. In Maine we see victims of hardscrabble and irredeemable ignorance lining up for anesthetic sales at Wal-Mart; and we see niche humans attempting to stay the flood, quaint wee Ozymandiases creating small deserts where once there was a world. And as Maine goes, so goes the nation. Driving through this beleaguered state of the Union, one tends to think that there is nobody left to do any of the things that might be done, that the sooner the emptied seas (only lobsters are left now off the coast; all the fish are dead) sweep over Maine the sooner the crustaceans will be able to sort out the crap.

Across the dying ocean, in England, in the heart of London, it is possible to see something else. The street markets of Camden Town are certainly full of the British version of the victims of hardscrabble—waves of astonishingly, irretrievably ill-educated and visibly unhealthy boys and girls in short-term employment looking for vendors to cheat them, elixir searchers galore in pursuit of the right poison, legal or illegal. Like anywhere. But it is also possible—which it is not in Maine, yet—to see Oscars, trickster prototypes.

It may be yet another chimera, but somehow it *seems* possible to see future-surfers in Camden Town. Not necessarily the cold-eyed, impossibly dexterous young adults on Rollerblades—though at times dozens of them can be seen simultaneously, threading their way through hordes of the visible victims of gravity, the toilers in the desuetude of urban life at the end of the twentieth century; at these times the Rollerbladers seem like visitors from another time. And not necessarily the users of mobile phones—far more frequently found in Camden Town than almost anywhere else in the world—their faces displaying whole harlequinades of animation as they gaze offstage, performing air kisses and clown frowns in a totally imaginary interaction with the invisible person they're speaking to. It may indeed be that these mobile-phone actors represent a foretaste of social interaction in the next century, that fifty years down the line, in Oscar's time, it won't matter who sees you, or what you do while others can watch, or what words they can hear you speak as long as the context of those words is not known; what will be utterly verboten will be to overhear both sides of a conversation. In a world increasingly indifferent to nakedness and to all the exposures of the body and soul that nakedness to others can entail, being overheard will be the ultimate invasion of privacy, because the words you use with another person are the words of your own private story. According to the implications of this speculative model, the dancers of the future will exhibit a postmillennium abhorrence of being overheard, because they will no longer be able to tolerate the thought of being caught in a bad story, a bad way of telling themselves who they are.

The millennium is a bad story.

What Oscar shares with sound-bite children talking into the air of Camden Town, almost certainly, is a sense that to be linked to one's past is the same as being caught in an undertow and drowned.

The past is a hook in the foot. It is an old story.

The past drags you under.

For the survivors next century, the past is utterly private. The continuity between you and any other human being is utterly private. In the next century, anything that can be seen or touched or heard is part of the information of the world. It is that which others spin so *they* can stay afloat. Oscar and his siblings (who inhabit Camden Town today) do not allow themselves visibly to obey the information of the world. They do not allow themselves to be caught in the bad stories we of this century told ourselves in order to avoid facing the realities to come.

The bad story of the millennium, a corrosive falsehood that eats away at the body politic, will do much to discredit the old world's versions of reality; it will privatize the lives of the streetwise; it will be so embarrassing to remember that, possibly, we of the affluent West will never join together again, with one heart and voice, to await universal disillusion.

A final few augurs from 1999 of what is

going to be survivor behavior:

Show Faces

In the 1990s two kinds of "nonfiction" television became increasingly popular: the self-exposing confessional interview/chat show (a format made popular by Oprah Winfrey, who announced her retirement early in 1999 out of disgust with the violence and psychotic intensities displayed by the kind of people who appeared on her show and its competitors) and the fake documentary (the documentary in which, with the compliance of the filmmakers or not, men and women pretend on film to be creatures they are not, or are filmed engaging in activities that are entirely staged). In England, the relatively (but decreasingly) prestigious Channel Four network recently screened a documentary about the odd relationship between a father and his daughter. Afterward, it was revealed (by the woman's real father) that the guy who claimed to be her father was really her boyfriend. The filmmakers' response was not to wilt like salted snails or to rear in astonished moral anguish, but to make a *new* documentary about the hoax couple, in order to find out how and why they faked their relationship.

It would be very surprising to find that the new documentary actually discovered anything about the twenty-first century. But I do think it's pretty clear that behavior such as this couple's—who were faced, as all of us are, with a media environment that deliberately muffles any distinction between "real" and "faked"—is profoundly adaptive. They, and the soi-disant psychotics who strike the fear of God into talk-show hostesses, are like lungfish. They may not do breathing awfully well, but they stick to the beach. They are learning to surf the new air.

They are spin-doctoring their own selves.

It may strike us—more accurately, it may strike those of us over the age of twenty—that this kind of behavior represents far more of a loss than any possible gain. And we may be right. *But who are we to bitch?* It is we, and our fathers and mothers, and their fathers and mothers, who sat supine in our boomer niches, in our Maines and Colorados and Oregons and Arizonas, and *let it happen*. We are the ones who rode blindfolded into the maelstrom of a world we had helped to degrade; we are the ones who bred children (usually out of vanity or carelessness) and set them loose to ride blindfolded a few paces further; and we should not be too chagrined if they are beginning to balk at committing suicide.

It is going to be a pretty terrible world down the chute from now. It is not going to be a world that is very kind to the likes of us, we guys and gals who grew so accustomed, as boomers, to thinking we owned the world and the means of expressing the world. Because all the time we were carving our thousand Rushmores in our own images upon a thousand wounded extrusions of the spoiled planet, the world we were born in was dying *of us*.

Time to spin.

Slam

For some time now, in New York and other metropolitan areas, a new cross between poetry and sung performance has become popular. "Poetry slams" are sessions in which a poet stands in front of an audience and performs his poetry in the form of a rap *tirade* (a French remark). The poet may be a singer or not, black or not, male or female. The poem is almost certainly ad-libbed. The audience is likely to be multiracial. The message conveyed will normally be political, or refer to racial, male-female, marital, or generational strife.

Transgression of norms is pleasurable; it marks off the transgressor as special, daring. But he or she is also, in this political theory of bodily extremity, a kind of cultural guerrilla, a harbinger of an imagined better future. The tattooed or pierced person has always been motivated by the pleasure of being different, of having permanently altered the virgin body in a manner both socially unacceptable and painful. Now the motive expands from the merely narcissistic to embrace a form of cultural revolt.

—MARK KINGWELL, *DREAMS OF MILLENNIUM: REPORT FROM A CULTURE ON THE BRINK*

Almost invariably, the rapped poem will constitute an assault upon those who are listening to it—or, rather, not so much an assault as a pantomime. Given the rate at which it is delivered and the constant noise typically generated by the audience, the slam poem can be seen as a way of expressing a body to the world. It represents a stance of the body in the world. It is not dissimilar to the dance of Rollerbladers through the crowds of Camden Town. Both convey a precarious sense of enablement; they both say to the world,

I am enabled to breathe this air. Look at my blades.

Listen to the rate of my words.

I ride on the blades.

I ride on the rap.

An interesting film of a few years ago, *Little Nemo: Adventures in Slumberland* (1993), did moderately well—surprisingly well, perhaps, given the fact that it was a cartoon rendering of a famous American strip from the turn of the last century made by a diverse group of multinational filmmakers, including Japanese animators, British animation consultants, American voices, and so forth. They took Winsor McCay's ornate urban vision of an America to come and translated it—very literally at times—into an elegy.

Like *Return to Oz* (1985), a deeply undervalued sequel to *The Wizard of Oz* (1939), *Little Nemo* is a late-century take on the prescience of the dreamers of a century ago—for it is certainly the case that both McCay and L. Frank Baum some-how captured the fever of the world to come, and McCay did quite clearly see the fever as malarial. His original comic strip is an astonishing vision of an America falling into hectic slumber, a slumber he seems to identify with the onslaught of the new century. Like the comic strip, the film is replete with implements, gadgets, solutions to mechanical problems that look like the wet dreams of Thomas Alva Edison (some would say the twentieth century as a whole is such a dream), and a powerful emphasis on Slumberland—which in the comic and the film is a land of dreams that may magically be visited by the seemingly awake Little Nemo—as a locale for the liberation of the psyche.

As the film develops, it becomes clear that there is a darker side of Slumberland—it continues to exist only as an epiphe-nomenon of the repressive unilateral tyranny of the devil-like ruler of Nightmareland, which exists "below" Slumberland, on the other side of a locked door that must not be opened. It is this fragile wonderland that Little Nemo visits in his long dream of the new century. He finds King Morpheus, who gives him a magic key that can open any door in the kingdom except the one door bearing the sigil that is also inscribed on the face of the key itself—that is, the door to the repressed, which wears a sigil face, a mirror, turned toward the world. That which is repressed, in other words, cannot unlock itself without external help.

Little Nemo seems initially disinclined to serve as the awakener of wonderland from the narcosis of its state, but he makes a friend, whose name is Flip. Flip, who boasts a raven familiar, is a trickster—he's a trickster in the original comic as well—and without his anarchic behavior, this state of uneasy repression would never be solved. But Flip the trickster inveigles Little Nemo to go exploring, and though it is Little Nemo himself who stumbles upon the door, after being washed down a vast dark staircase, it is the trickster who persuades him to open the door and to unbind the devil.

The devil then invades the light (which he empowers in any case) and drags King Morpheus back down to Nightmareland.

But Little Nemo now takes responsibility for the actions his own anarchic id has led him into, and restores balance to the world of dreams. He creates a twentieth-century America anyone would be proud to live in. Having entrapped the devil-shaped king of Nightmareland in something that is half mushroom cloud and half Max Ernst rendering of Babel, he returns to his own Manhattan, which (after he "wakes") is suddenly filled with joy.

For the clowns have come, and the revels, and the circus.

Would it had been so.

Vulture,
When you come for the white rat that the foxes left,
Take off the red helmet of your head, the black
Wings that have shadowed me, and step to me as man:
The wild brother at whose feet the white wolves fawn,
To whose hand of power the great lioness
Stalks, purring . . .
You know what I was,
You see what I am: change me, change me!

—RANDALL JARRELL, "THE WOMAN AT THE WASHINGTON ZOO"

What happened, in the real world, was Henry Ford.

It is such a tragedy. America is a thousand frontiers, a million boundaries, and always has been. It is the home of the confidence man—the nineteenth-century version of the spin doctor, who, underneath the paint, is a trickster. Everyone moves all the time in America. Everyone crosses boundaries, cons new communities into believing tall tales about their past. Everyone confabulates in America. It is the true land of the trickster—but its citizens cannot admit the case.

If the confidence man is one of America's unacknowledged founding fathers, then instead of saying that there are no modern tricksters one could argue the opposite: trickster is everywhere. To travel from place to place in the ancient world was not only unusual, it was often taken to be a sign of mental derangement. . . , but now everyone travels. If by "America" we mean the land of rootless wanderers and the free market, the land not of natives but of immigrants, the shameless land where anyone can say anything at any time, the land of opportunity and therefore of opportunists, the land where individuals are allowed and even encouraged to act without regard to community, then trickster has not disappeared. "America" is his apotheosis; he's pandemic.

—LEWIS HYDE, *TRICKSTER MAKES THE WORLD*

Tricksters and monotheism don't mix, after all.

**THERE ARE
NO SERVICES
ON THIS ROUTE.**

—ROAD SIGN

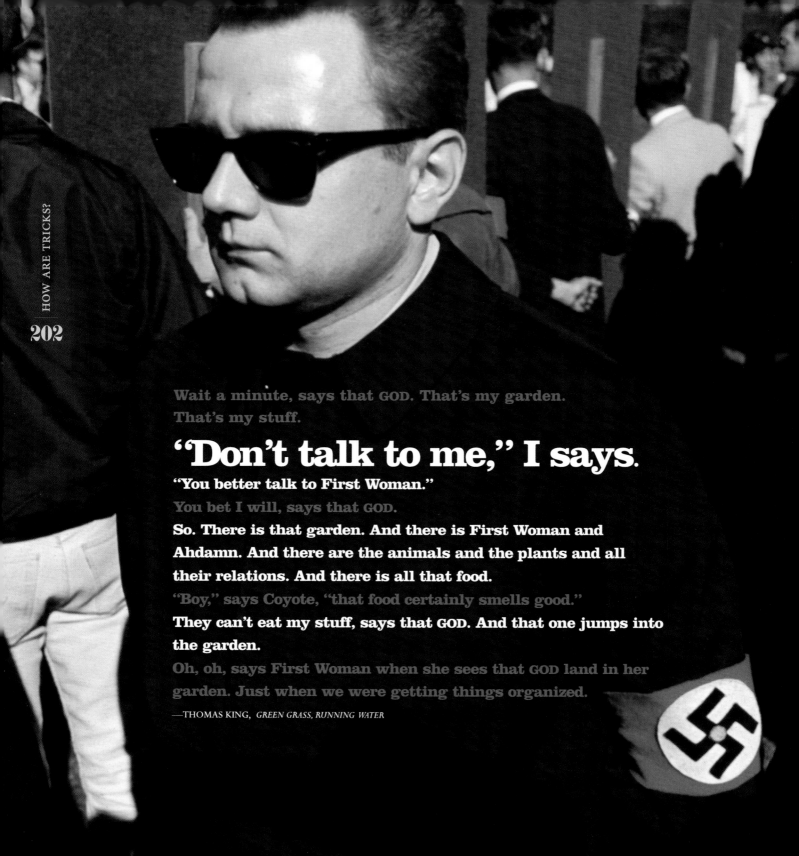

Wait a minute, says that GOD. That's my garden.
That's my stuff.

"Don't talk to me," I says.

"You better talk to First Woman."

You bet I will, says that GOD.

So. There is that garden. And there is First Woman and
Ahdamn. And there are the animals and the plants and all
their relations. And there is all that food.

"Boy," says Coyote, "that food certainly smells good."

They can't eat my stuff, says that GOD. And that one jumps into
the garden.

Oh, oh, says First Woman when she sees that GOD land in her
garden. Just when we were getting things organized.

—THOMAS KING, *GREEN GRASS, RUNNING WATER*

So perhaps there is a reason for the fixated pallor Americans see in their mirrors, the theme-park glares of hysterics caught in a floodlight when they refuse the dance of tomorrow.

The reason is that Americans have refused to admit that they are the great confidence artists of the Western world.

The trouble is that around about 1920, they began to believe their own sermons.

While in this state of amnesia, they did more than any other nation to destroy the planet that sustains us all but may not continue doing so.

So it is time for a message to the West.
Wake up.
Everyone is in the best seat.

—JOHN CAGE

Wake up into the dream.

So, instead of trying to dance as we travel down the road to Armageddon, or mourn as we are marched off to someone else's utopia, let us sit awhile and tell our stories. And let us be prepared to listen to others' stories. For that way, maybe, we can travel on, not to Armageddon, nor even to utopia, but on Holy Pilgrimage to a destination not within our control, thank God.

—MARTIN PALMER, *DANCING TO ARMAGEDDON*

It is going to be a terrible new century.

But if we don't learn to surf it, if we don't learn to keep our privacy and our integrity intact in the fractal badlands ahead, then we're dead. If we don't learn how to surf the darkness and the chaos, we're dead.

Mistah Kurtz—he dead.

—JOSEPH CONRAD, "HEART OF DARKNESS"

So, please.
Please, Americans.
Trick us again, Flip, Coyote, Oscar.

Trick us through the bad nights to come.

PARABOLA: Is there a need to purge the memory, and because of that the apocalyptic idea comes to the surface? I'm fascinated with the idea of a people who can do without history.

UKL: Haven't most of us largely done without history? As I understand, most people before modern industrial culture did not have a history for longer than a couple of generations. They had stories about the year the stars fell, or they kept a year count, like the Lakota, which might go back fifty or sixty years, but not much longer. And before that was dreamtime, was mythtime. Is that time really "before"? Or is it "the other time"?

PARABOLA: Yes, as Eliade speaks of, *in illo tempore*. Or faerie time.

UKL: Very frequently in Native American world pictures, there is a dreamtime, the other time, in which, for one thing, people and animals are absolutely not distinguished. All beings are of the same order. And then comes the change, when, as in the Yurok stories for instance, it's quite clear that time alters. Coyote says things like "when we come to the time of change, when the people take over." Now there's a millennium for you! Not in the sense of a thousand years, but in the sense of an absolute change into a different kind of time. There's a time when they're getting the world ready, and then there's the time when the inheritors, the human people, take over.

—URSULA K. LE GUIN, INTERVIEW PUBLISHED IN *PARABOLA*

In the desert
I saw a creature, naked, bestial,
Who, squatting upon the ground,
Held his heart in his hands,
And ate of it.
I said, "Is it good, friend?"
"It is bitter—bitter," he answered;
"But I like it
Because it is bitter,
And because it is my heart."

—STEPHEN CRANE, POEM III

And God said unto Noah,

"The end of all flesh is come before me; for the earth is filled with violence through them; and, behold, I will destroy them with the earth . . . and I will cause it to rain upon the earth forty days and forty nights; and every living substance that I have made I will destroy from off the face of the earth."

—GENESIS 6:13, 7:4

The Ark, Gustave Doré

IV

THE FACE OF THE WORLD

Life's a long tragedy; this globe's the stage.

—ISAAC WATTS, *EPISTLE TO MITIO*

The Flood as we know it is a neatly told story—the versions attributed to the scribes now known as J and P have been woven together almost seamlessly into the Bible we are familiar with—and it has long been understood by Christians of earlier centuries as a story that is a prefiguring or "type" of the end of the world. The tale is easy to understand in this fashion; in the climate of the late twentieth century, almost fatally easy. God or Yahweh sees the sinfulness of all flesh, and is outraged; he determines to end the world; and except for Noah (who prefigures Christ) and his family, he does precisely that. The ark becomes a rapture cart. Only the saved, in other words, are saved; the arena of earth drowns in corpses.

It is a great story, but even some Christians may have found it difficult to sort out the God of this great story—a vengeful, entirely terrifying deity who comes to a seemingly irrevocable clear-cut decision based on ponderings we have no access to, and who simultaneously sneaks diagrams to Noah so he can build an ark (or big box, a translation closer to the original meaning) to save himself along with breeding stock, plus a few extra animals to sacrifice to the Lord after the Flood has subsided.

The problem with the biblical story of Noah and the Flood is that it attempts to conflate two gods. There is the vengeful destroyer, and there is the cunning giver of good advice to humans. These gods do not mix well, even under the overriding moral imperatives that govern J's and P's versions.

They do not mix; and at this late hour, as we slide into the procrustean jaws of the millennium we have fabricated out of the literalism of our faith and the anxiety in our hearts, it might be worthwhile casting an eye back at the original Mesopotamian story, which first came to the Western world's notice in the nineteenth century, when Tablet IX of the Gilgamesh myth was first deciphered, and which has been deepened for our eyes since the translation of the Atrahasis story in 1956.

The parallels are most obvious in the Atrahasis version. The chief god, Enlil, grows weary of the noise humans make and decides to obliterate them by causing a great flood to inundate the earth. But Enki (who is called Prometheus in Ovid's version of the story) resists Enlil's decree by advising Atrahasis how to build a boat. Atrahasis does so, loading it with a wide range of animals. He finds out whether the flood has subsided by sending out birds to check.

The differences are just as great. There is no moral imperative. The gods, as a whole, are stupid and vindictive— a characteristic of most gods in most mythologies. Only Enki, the friend of humans, is clever. And if we continue to the end of the story, these differences only increase: After the seeming destruction of all life, the gods begin to suffer because there's no one around to feed them. Joy is almost unbounded, therefore, when Enki reveals the survival of Atrahasis—but Enlil is still enraged because there will soon be too many humans again, making altogether too much noise. So Enki arranges to make some women barren, and to enact other birth control measures. Humanity from then on will not overcrowd the world, and the gods will not take vengeance on them.

Enki is, of course, a trickster god. The solution he suggests for the world's woes is radically at odds with the kinds of solutions offered by the "advanced" religions of the twentieth century; he represents the kind of mind-set that, had polytheism prevailed, might have helped humanity shape myths that expressed a more complex admiration of our species than do the demonizing unilateral tales we grew up with in the real West.

If we need any god in these latter days, Enki is the kind of god we need.

But the trickster needs a habitation, and he needs borderlands. He needs a world that we may not any longer be able to imagine, because our visions of the future have become defined by formulations of things to come that have an unutterably disastrous effect on the human spirit.

Alas for these latter days! The world had grown old, and all its inmates partook of the decrepitude. Why talk of infancy, manhood, and old age? We all stood equal sharers of the last throes of time-worn nature.

—MARY SHELLEY, *THE LAST MAN*

There is the invert world of virtual reality, which amounts to little more than the insertion of an indefinite regressive series of theme parks into our head by electronic means. There are theme parks themselves, which amount to a vision of America as a great babushka doll of gated communities, gated jobs, gated malls, all sorted inside one another till you reach the center, which is hollow. There is the future that heroes and villains flee from in sf movies. There is heat death. There is global warming till the seas choke with dead algae.

And there are the woebegone landscapes of the Revelation of St. John the Divine,

I saw four angels standing on the four corners of the earth, holding the four winds of the earth, that the wind should not blow on the earth, nor on the sea, nor on any tree.

And I saw another angel ascending from the east, having the seal of the living God; and he cried with a loud voice to the four angels, to whom it was given to hurt the earth and the sea.

Saying, Hurt not the earth, neither the sea, nor the trees, till we have sealed the servants of our God in their foreheads.

—REVELATIONS 7:1–3

which are preserved as an arena for the unfolding of the sacred drama only until the virtuous have had their foreheads stenciled with "Good for Rapture" seals.

After that, let the fire fall.

My son has been a subscriber to your magazine for a couple of years, but until this morning I had never actually bothered to read it myself. Even though I have never been very interested in wildlife, I thought it was a harmless enough subject, suitable for a 12-year-old. But when I looked inside the February issue today I was shocked. . . .[The writer then complains of the acceptance of evolution in the articles.] I was also dismayed to see that you also seem to have an implicit allegiance to that other heresy, Environmentalism, which puts Nature above Man and is thus no different from witchcraft or voodoo. God gave Man a mind so that he could control Nature. He also gave Man a limited time on earth before the Day of Judgement. Environmentalism attempts to postpone that day—Armageddon—and this is sacrilege.

—LETTER IN THE APRIL 1989 *BBC WILDLIFE* MAGAZINE

Above right: *Annunciation and Saints (detail)*, Francia II

None of these is a world for the trickster.
They are not, any of them,
worlds human beings should be asked to live in.

So perhaps we should look at the face of the world in another way.

Another kind of story about the nature of the heart of the
world we were born into does come to mind.

One world at a time.
—HENRY DAVID THOREAU

There is a bitter tang at the heart of this story as well, and ironies, and inconsistencies: but that is what we want, I think, if we are to contemplate ourselves as aspiring after the trickster, the master of spin, the bringer of fire: Prometheus bringing fire down and stinging our fingers with fire, forcing us to lick our fingers in order to soothe them. That which is bitter can taste sweet on the tongue. The burn heals and we have fire.

But we need a vision of the world, even if it makes us wry-necked. The world is all we've got.

> The grave's a fine and private place,
> But none, I think, do there embrace. . . .
> Let us roll all our strength, and all
> Our sweetness up into one ball;
> And tear our pleasures with rough strife
> Thorough the iron gates of life,
> Thus, though we cannot make our sun
> Stand still, yet we will make him run.
>
> —ANDREW MARVELL, "TO HIS COY MISTRESS"

It is an intolerably complex place to imagine and, in the end, intolerably cruel to inhabit, because every single one of us, up to now—with the exception of a few astronauts caught in the upper atmosphere—have died here. The world is where we begin and where we end.

It is, or should be, sacred.

> And did those feet in ancient time
> Walk upon Englands mountains green:
> And was the Holy Lamb of God,
> On England's pleasant pastures seen
>
> And did the Countenance Divine
> Shine forth upon our clouded hills?
> And was Jerusalem builded here
> Among these dark Satanic Mills?
>
> Bring me my Bow of burning gold:
> Bring me my Arrows of desire:
> Bring me my Spear: O clouds unfold!
> Bring me my Chariot of fire!
>
> I will not cease from Mental Fight,
> Nor shall my Sword sleep in my hand,
> Till we have built Jerusalem,
> In Englands green & pleasant Land.
>
> —WILLIAM BLAKE, "A NEW JERUSALEM"

Top: *Last Judgement* (detail), Hans Memling

They wept for humanity, those two, not for themselves. They could not bear that this should be the end. Ere silence was completed their hearts were opened, and they knew what had been important on the earth. Man, the flower of all flesh, the noblest of all creatures visible, man who had once made god in his image, and had mirrored his strength on the constellations, beautiful naked man was dying, strangled in the garments he had woven. Century after century had he toiled, and here was his reward. Truly the garment had seemed heavenly at first, shot with the colours of culture, sewn with the threads of self-denial. And heavenly it had been so long as it was a garment and no more, so long as man could shed it at will and live by the essence that is his soul, and the essence, equally divine, that is his body. The sin against the body—it was for that they wept in chief; the centuries of wrong against the muscles and the nerves, and those five portals by which we can alone apprehend—glozing it over with talk of evolution, until the body was white pap, the home of ideas colourless, last sloshy stirrings of a spirit that had grasped the stars.

—E. M. FORSTER, "THE MACHINE STOPS"

It is intolerably complex, soiled and sealed with a thousand seals that Solomon might have blessed, succulent and more wrinkled than the neck of the most ancient of crones; it shrinks and shrivels under the deathly touch, the halitosis breath, of the fundamentalists who hope to help the millennium in; it is death to the touch in the end, and it is fun. It is fun.

It is the place of all the fun we're going to have.

So we need to loosen up our vision of this world. We need to put some flesh and incongruity back into our sense of where we do our lives, some sense that the world is more complex than the bee's-eye vision of things we get by surfing TV channels or the Model T nightmares of these primitive days of the Internet, that it is richer than what we can see from the interstates we spend—if we are Americans—so much of our lives being obedient to. [We should not forget that what the interstate system has done to America, and what its equivalents are doing to all the other "advanced" countries of the Western world, is to radically simplify the experiences and choices of those who use it. Any intersection on the interstate is any other intersection; any shopping mall is all shopping malls, the same Astroturf domes whose towers blind the stars: the same, the same. For a person who is not American, perhaps the most astonishing aspect of American life in 1999—though it is so ubiquitous it is almost invisible—is the sight of 250 million Americans obeying a grid of roads, shaping their lives around a bunch of *roads*. (A survey done in Washington, D.C., according to its director, Roy Kienitz, claims that Americans spend something like 40 percent more time behind the wheel than they did in 1990; a typical mother drives twenty-nine miles daily, making five journeys.)]

So a map of the interstate system is all too simple to live by, even though many of us, in practical terms, almost do so already. Indeed, the realities that system simplifies are themselves too simple to live with—which is one of the reasons America has become the world corporate heart of the disappointment-management industry. A map of the interstate system is a route to hell. If we are going to spin into a new world beyond the dire simplicities we impose on things—but constantly and inevitably failing to allay the anxieties that gnaw us, no matter how hysterically we displace our fears into demons only mental patients or fundamentalists could credit in daylight—we need a map of the world to hold in our minds and hearts, a chart corresponding to our needs for a richness of view, a complexity of venue to shape our lives within.

I would suggest the mappemonde (or mappa mundi; the two terms may be used interchangeably).

Definition

Mappemonde: From here to home as the trickster flies.

If by mappemonde what we first mean is a storylike portrait of a region sacred to a particular folk—a definition consistent with formal analyses of the mappemonde as a pictorial/narrative vision of the world known to medieval Christians—then we are getting somewhere.

There have, of course, been maps of the world in existence for a very long time, some of them far more "accurate" than the mappemonde, which comes late in the history of cartography. The ancient Middle East, in particular, housed several civilizations capable of generating highly potent symbolic representations of the world in which they lived. These maps were not "accurate," as we understand the term; they served rather as evocations—profoundly evocative iconic images—of the meaning of the world around them, *tableaux vivants* that incorporated the significant shape of the sacred dramas central to these civilizations. These maps were generally circular, and around the central region, which was both the heart of the world and the heart of the map, they typically deployed a complex pattern of images featuring emblematic figures of gods and beasts and men, often drawn with cartoonlike clarity, performing sacred symbolic deeds. Images emblematic of earth and water and sky would also be visible in this frieze. A vast snake or dragon might encircle the central images. And an explanatory text would weave through the images, connecting disparate elements and scales and memories into a kind of trail, the kind of trail Odysseus (son and grandson of trickster figures, and a trickster in his own right) might have left as he inscribed his uncanny boustrophedons unendingly across wine-dark seas, through the water margins of the great earth, until the final crossroads.

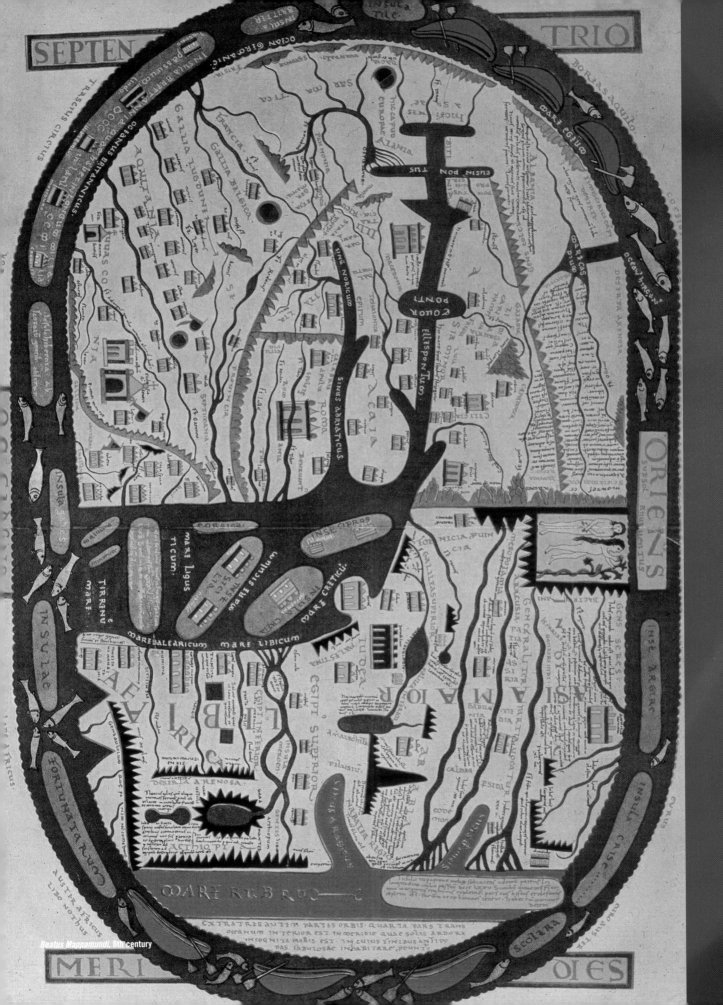

Beatus Mappamundi, 8th century

In the end, an ancient world map would not much resemble anything we might think of as a map. To modern eyes, it would look more like a medallion or an astrological sigil, of the sort that might be worn around the neck of a priest or priestess.

It would look as though it was meant to be *told*. It would look as though it was a multitude of stories looking to be told at once.

So the ancient map was a cosmology, not a chart—a vade mecum, not a list of exits on the interstate. It was not intended to direct travelers; its job was to direct lives. If there were road maps in the ancient world, they were used to extinction many centuries ago.

(It is almost impossible now, in 1999, to find road maps of America that predate World War II. They too have been used to extinction.)

There were maps of the world in ancient Greece, too; and after six centuries of thought and mathematics and mea-surement, Ptolemy (90–168) created the first world map whose features we might recognize as pertaining to our round globe. But Ptolemy's version of the world soon disappeared. It was of very little interest to the Christian fathers, who preserved only those aspects of the old world they felt to be not irredeemably pagan. Much, of course, was lost. The golden lads and girls of the olden world were turned to dust. And although the mappemondes that followed were humanly richer than Ptolemy's quantity survey of the world, only those who refuse knowledge could argue that the mappemonde was actually *better* than a map navigators wouldn't kill themselves trying to follow. So no actual map drawn by Ptolemy survives, though the Ptolemaic maps we're familiar with, those drawn by late-fifteenth-century Renaissance cartographers, are based on his theoretical writings. These scholars did not sim-ply paste a prestigious ancient name to their own speculative work.

In the meantime, however, something else had happened.

The record is very patchy: The Christian monks of the Dark Ages, snuggled into damp monasteries without proper windows and no temperature control systems, were not remarkably retentive of written or inscribed material from previous ages (then again, modern publishers routinely shred their own backlists; there is nothing new under the sun). But the record does seem to hint that world maps so constructed as to tell a story—maps far less accurate than the classical maps attributed to Ptolemy et alia—did not come back into full cultural existence until about the time the first millennium itself began to be conceived, retroactively, with a whole false-memory historiogra-

phy climaxing in the year 1000. Not until the twelfth or thirteenth century, then, did it seem necessary to attempt to encompass the world in the Christian story, to create mappemondes indurated with that divine version.

Over and above systemic failures of retention throughout the world of Europe, world maps as a category must have had a very low priority in the archives of the Dark Ages interregnum. They almost certainly conveyed an air of unwholesomeness for the early Christian mentality, fixed as it was upon an early resolution of the drama of the Second Coming, for the Ptolemaic world map focused altogether too cogently on a world that was secular and measurable. Ptolemy cast too much light, with an all-too-unholy pagan focus, in the wrong direction. He saw a world the Christians were bound to despise. The survival of post-Ptolemaic maps in the Dark Ages was chancy. The survival of Ptolemaic maps was not. There was no chance at all.

No ancient map has survived from antiquity.

The earliest Ptolemaic manuscript has its origin in the thirteenth century; the first Latin translation of his works seems to have been in 1406, though he was in print from 1477. Renaissance Ptolemaic maps are reconstructions from his texts. They are remarkable for the fact that they are *not* manifestly stories of the world or graphic encyclopedias; they are "just" maps.

They are signals of a post-Christian world. They are triumphs of the human mind, and their ultimate fate—which is to signal exits on the interstate—should not vitiate our sense of how miraculous were the processes of deduction and measurement necessary for them to become what they have.

But they did not manifest the labyrinth of trampolines—the trampoline of labyrinths—where the trickster makes his home.

The Christian mappemonde, which is first encountered in the sixth century and which came to full flower in medieval times, is first and foremost a conscious illustration of the Bible—which is a narrative—and takes its general shape from chapters 9 and 10 of Genesis, which recount how the world was divided among the three sons of Noah. The medieval world map is therefore tripartite.

But in their attempts to tell the biblical story, the creators of the mappemonde clearly end up telling more than one story simultaneously—secular, religious, navigational, and political lines of narrative constantly interpenetrate. These stories need not be—and indeed are almost certainly not—mutually consistent. As Peter Whitfield says in *The Image of the World: Twenty Centuries of World Maps* (1994):

Untitled (Shark), David Wojnarowicz

Death, One of the Four Riders from the Apocalypse, Polde Limbourg

The essential unity and seriousness of purpose which we would expect from a world map is absent. The contemporary parallel that comes to mind is the medieval mystery play: religious in origin, but also satirical, improvisatory, flouting the unities of time and place, and functioning on several different levels to present a powerful, dramatic but not a logical coherent picture of the world.

Whenever Peter Whitfield talks about the mappemonde, he could as easily be talking about the undertext of the Revelation of St. John the Divine, for they are both structures that attempt to contain superfluxes of story—story upon story—whose complexities and mutual inconsistencies baffle the senses. Revelation, after all, makes very little sense as a single story. Rather, it is a pomegranate of story whose readers pluck from it the seeds they need, the seeds they (if they are fundamentalist) tend to think of as the one and holy seed of God's story. What we tend to think of as the real world—because we are used to thinking the world is coterminous with the visions of the descendants of Ptolemy—is, seen through the multiple filters of Revelation or the mappemonde, so many simultaneous visions that our first instinct is to recoil from the chaos. We correctly discount the surface story—in Revelation it is the story of the end times; in the mappemonde it is a rendering of the world as a revelation of the Bible as a whole—but we miss the utility of that seeming chaos.

What the mappemonde gives us is a vision of the world as something more complex than any map that measures distance could ever convey. The mappemonde is a cauldron of story. All unconscious of the effect of their attempts to integrate this blessed and unholy potpourri into one story, the makers of the mappemonde gave us the symbolic representation of a world that contains us all, which contains in its secret caverns the lucubrations—the midnight oil—of all our dreams. All the spoons of the world could stir the mappemonde and not reach the bottom of the pot.

It cannot be made sense of. It is omnivorous. It will eat—it will make its own sense of—any fact. It mocks the simplistic devouring hysterias that mark the century we are leaving as one whose inhabitants had not yet gotten used to the new worlds their own tools were helping to create. It is as close to a map of the Internet as anything we're likely to generate on our own. It is a home for tricksters.

Mappemonde chugalugs chaos neat.

So we should hang mappemondes on the walls of our cave as 1999 turns to 2000, and the Y2K geek goof begins to wreak chaos (or not), and a new day dawns.

How lucky for us, perhaps, to be here.

Out of mist, God's
Blind hand gropes to find
Your face. The fingers
Want to memorize your face. The fingers
Will be wet with the tears of your eyes. God

Wants only to love you, perhaps.

—ROBERT PENN WARREN, "INTERJECTION #6: WHAT YOU SOMETIMES FEEL ON YOUR FACE AT NIGHT"

Hunt, hunt again. If you do not find it, you
Will die. But I tell you this much, it
Is not under the stone at the foot
Of the garden, nor by the wall by the fig tree.
I tell you this much to save you trouble, for I
Have looked, I know. But hurry, for

The terror is, all promises are kept.
Even happiness.

—ROBERT PENN WARREN, "TREASURE HUNT"

We are lucky, after all, to be alive. Here we are at the end of time, which may mean no more than saying that we have done with one history, and must begin another. It is entirely possible, too, that we are at the end of the world. Let us assume that we are not, for the moment. Let us assume that it will be possible for us to spin the world that is left.

Let us assume that, chastened and ribald and irreverent and streetwise and kind at last to the lives we share and husband, we can begin to spin and span, take and tickle that which remains.

Fat chance? Only chance.

In our end is our beginning. Let us sit in the caves of the dark, with our illuminated manuscripts in our hands. Let us make jokes.

Super Powers, Howard Finster

Time does not repair.
Time is irreparable.

—*THE LITTLE BOOK OF APHORISMS OF THE END*

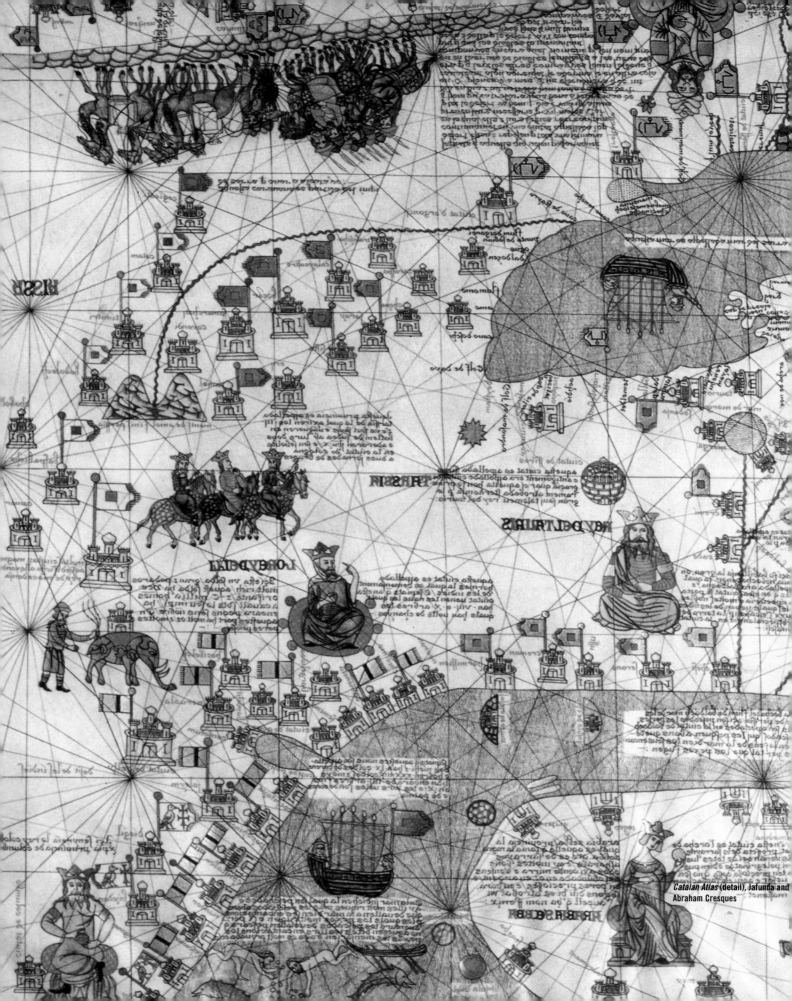

Catalan Atlas (detail), Jafunda and Abraham Cresques

We are for the dark. We will die in the dark. But the dark is where we were born.

A wind rose, and a wind fell,
And the day that was that day
Hung against a turning sun....

A wind rose, and a wind fell,
And the day that was that day
Vanished in the darkness.
—AMY LOWELL, "THE DAY THAT WAS THAT DAY"

As we burn the midnight oil of the world.

I sate myself down for some tim musing sorrowfully; then I rose and took my way with slow foot steps towards the place in which heard the sounds of men.

—EDWARD BULWER LYTTON, *THE COMING RACE*

Ho, Eve! my grey carrion wife,
When we have supped on king's marrow,
Where shall we drink and make merry our lif
Our nest it is queen Cleopatra's skull,
'Tis cloven and crack'd,
And batter'd and hack'd,
But with tears of blue eyes it is full:
Let us drink then, my raven of Cairo!

—THOMAS LOVELL BEDDOES, "THE SONG THAT WOLFRAM HEARD IN HELL"

mean, after all; you have to consider we're only made
ut of dust. That's admittedly not much to go on and we
houldn't forget that. But even considering, I mean it's
 sort of bad beginning, we're not doing too bad. So I
ersonally have faith that even in this lousy situation
ve're faced with we can make it. You get me?

—PHILIP K. DICK, *THE THREE STIGMATA OF PALMER ELDRITCH*

Over!
Over! and
that is the end
of all stories.

—HANS CHRISTIAN ANDERSEN, "THE FIR-TREE"

Nuclear Winter, Roger Brown

ART CREDITS

111 Jerry Ohlingers, NY, still from *The Spawn*
112 Jerry Ohlingers, NY, still from *8 ½*
115 Jerry Ohlingers, NY, still from *Forbidden Planet*
117 Corbis/Bettmann, Joseph Sohm
118 Jerry Ohlingers, NY, stills from *Dr. Strangelove*
121 The Everett Collection
122 Jerry Ohlingers, NY, still from *The X-Files* TV series
124 Jerry Ohlingers, NY, still from *Millennium* TV series
128 Phyllis Kind Gallery, NY, *Actual Dream of the Second Coming*, Roger Brown
134 Phyllis Kind Gallery, NY, *Final Arbiter*, Roger Brown
137 Bridgeman Art Library/Richardson & Kailas Icons, Archangels Michael & Gabriel,
      10th or 11th century
140 Jerry Ohlingers, NY, still from *Ben Hur*
142 *Doonesbury* © G. B. Trudeau. Printed with permission of UNIVERSAL PRESS SYNDICATE, All Rights Reserved
143 Jerry Ohlingers, NY, still from *Cape Fear*
145 Jerry Ohlingers, NY, still from *Fahrenheit 451*
147 Jerry Ohlingers, NY, still from *Nightmare on Elm Street*
149 Jerry Ohlingers, NY, still from *Apocalypse Now*
150 The Everett Collection, stills from *Lord of the Rings*
152 Art Resource, Tate Gallery, *Death on a Pale Horse,* Joseph Mallord/William Turner
154 Corbis/Michael Maslan, Historic Photos; Archive Photos, center
155 Corbis/George Hall
159 Corbis/Mitchell Gerber
160 Jerry Ohlingers, NY, still from *The Texas Chainsaw Massacre*
165 Jerry Ohlingers, NY, still from *The Exorcist*
166 John Yeats/AK Press, San Francisco
169 Jerry Ohlingers, NY, still from *Things to Come*
170 Jerry Ohlingers, NY, still from *Alien*
171 Jerry Ohlingers, NY, still from *2001*
172 Jerry Ohlingers, NY, still from *Star Trek* TV series
174 Jerry Ohlingers, NY, still from *The Wizard of Oz*
175 Jerry Ohlingers, NY, still from *Blade Runner*
180 Jerry Ohlingers, NY, still from *Alien*
182 Jerry Ohlingers, NY, still from *Volcano*
186 Jerry Ohlingers, NY, still from *Batman*
189 Jerry Ohlingers, NY, stills from *The Ten Commandments* and *Gremlins*
191 Allen and Barry H, *Day of Victory*, McKendree Robbins Long
195 Corbis/Bettmann
199 Jerry Ohlingers, NY, stills from *Little Nemo's Adventures in Slumberland*
      and *The Wizard of Oz*
201 Jerry Ohlingers, NY, still from *Batman* TV series
202 Corbis/Leif Skoogfors
205 Jerry Ohlingers, NY, still from *Starship Troopers*
209 Phyllis Kind Gallery, *American Devils*, Howard Finster
211 Bridgeman Art Library/Pinacoteca Nazionale, Bologna, *Annunciation and Saints* (detail), Francia II
214 Scala/Art Resource, *Last Judgement* (detail), Hans Memling (top)
217 Bridgeman Art Library, *Beatus Mappamundi*, 8th century
219 Jerry Ohlingers, NY, still from *The Name of the Rose*
221 PPOW, New York, *Untitled (shark)*, David Wojnarowicz
222 Bridgeman Art Library, *Death, One of the Four Riders from the Apocalypse,* Polde Limbourg
225 Phyllis Kind Gallery, *Super Powers*, Howard Finster
229 Phyllis Kind Gallery, *Nuclear Winter*, Roger Brown

SELECTED BIBLIOGRAPHY

Abanes, Richard. *The Road to Armageddon?* New York: Four Walls Eight Windows, 1998.

Athanasiou, Tom. *Slow Reckoning: The Ecology of a Divided Planet.* London: Secker & Warburg, 1997.

Atwood, Margaret. *Strange Things: The Malevolent North in Canadian Literature.* Oxford: Clarendon Press, 1995.

Barton, Carlin A. *The Sorrows of the Ancient Romans: The Gladiator and the Monster.* Princeton: Princeton University Press, 1993.

Bernstein, Michael André. *Bitter Carnival: Ressentiment and the Abject Hero.* Princeton: Princeton University Press, 1992.

Bethea, David M. *The Shape of Apocalypse in Modern Russian Fiction.* Princeton: Princeton University Press, 1989.

Bloom, Harold. *Omens of Millennium: The Gnosis of Angels, Dreams, and Resurrection.* New York: Riverhead Books, 1996.

Boyer, Paul. *When Time Shall Be No More: Prophecy Belief in Modern American Culture.* Cambridge, MA: Harvard University Press, 1992.

Brown, Lester R., Christopher Flain, and Hilary French. *State of the World 1997: A Worldwatch Institute Report on Progress Toward a Sustainable Society.* New York: W.W. Norton & Company, 1997.

Brown, Lester R., Nicholas Lenssen, and Hale Kane. *Vital Signs: The Trends That Are Shaping Our Future.* New York: W.W. Norton & Company, 1995 and later.

Cendrars, Blaise. *Modernities & Other Writings.* Lincoln: University of Nebraska Press, 1992.

Cohn, Norman. *The Pursuit of the Millennium.* London: Secker & Warburg, 1957.

Daniel, Howard. *Devils, Monsters and Nightmares.* New York: Abelard-Schuman, 1957.

Dunant, Sarah and Roy Porter, eds. *The Age of Anxiety.* North Pomfret, VT: Virago Press, 1996.

Eco, Umberto. *Apocalypse Postponed.* Bloomington: Indiana University Press, 1994.

Ehrenfeld, David. *Beginning Again: People and Nature in the New Millennium.* New York: Oxford University Press, 1993.

Eichenberg, Fritz. *Dance of Death: A Graphic Commentary on the Danse Macabre Through the Centuries.* New York: Abbeville Press, 1983.

Garreau, Joel. *Edge City: Life on the New Frontier.* New York: Doubleday, 1991.

Gelernter, David. *1939: The Lost World of the Fair.* New York: The Free Press, 1995.

Gould, Stephen Jay. *Questioning the Millennium: A Rationalist's Guide to a Precisely Arbitrary Countdown.* London: Jonathan Cape, 1997.

Hewitt, V.J., and Peter Lorie. *Nostradamus: The End of the Millennium: Prophecies: 1992 to 2001.* London: Bloomsbury, 1991.

Hunter, Anthony. *The Last Days.* London: Anthony Blond, 1958.

Hyde, Lewis. *Trickster Makes the World: Mischief, Myth, and Art.* New York: Farrar, Straus & Giroux, 1998.

Kingwell, Mark. *Dreams of Millennium: Report from a Culture on the Brink.* Toronto: Viking, 1996.

Kossy, Donna. *Kooks: A Guide to the Outer Limits of Human Belief.* Los Angeles: Feral House, 1994.

Lattimore, Richmond, trans. *The Revelation of John.* New York: Harcourt, Brace & World, Inc., 1962.

Leakey, Richard, and Roger Lewin. *The Sixth Extinction: Patterns of Life and the Future of Mankind.* New York: Doubleday, 1995.

Lemesurier, Peter. *The Nostradamus Encyclopedia: The Definitive Reference Guide to the Work and World of Nostradamus.* New York: St. Martin's Press, 1997.

Leslie, John. *The End of the World: The Science and Ethics of Human Extinction.* New York: Routledge, 1996.

McGuinn, Bernard. *Anti-Christ: Two Thousand Years of the Human Fascination with Evil.* San Francisco: HarperSanFrancisco, 1994.

McKibben, Bill. *The Age of Missing Information.* New York: Random House, 1992.

McMenamin, Mark and Diana. *Hypersea: Life on Land*. New York: Columbia University Press, 1994.

Mann, A.T. *Millennium Prophecies: Predictions for the Year 2000*. Rockport, MA: Element Books, 1992.

Manuel, Frank E., ed. *Utopias and Utopian Thought: A Timely Appraisal*. Boston: Houghton Mifflin Company, 1966.

Naisbitt, John. *Megatrends Asia: Eight Asian Megatrends That Are Reshaping Our World*. New York: Simon & Schuster, 1996.

O'Leary, Stephen D. *Arguing the Apocalypse: A Theory of Millennial Rhetoric*. New York: Oxford University Press, 1994.

Palmer, Martin. *Dancing to Armageddon*. Aquarius/Thorsons, 1992.

Parfrey, Adam, ed. *Apocalypse Culture*. Los Angeles: Feral House, 1987, expanded 1990.

Petersen, Rodney L. *Preaching in the Last Days: The Theme of "Two Witnesses" in the Sixteenth and Seventeenth Centuries*. New York: Oxford University Press, 1993.

Roeseler, Karl, and David Gilbert, eds. *2000andwhat?* Berkeley, CA: Trip Street Press, 1996.

Roob, Alexander. *The Hermetic Museum: Alchemy & Mysticism*. Taschen, 1997.

Schwartz, Hillel. *Century's End: An Orientation Manual Toward the Year 2000*. New York: Doubleday, 1990; revised edition, 1996.

Shaw, Eva. *Eve of Destruction: Prophecies, Theories and Preparations for the End of the World*. Chicago: Contemporary Books, 1995.

Showalter, Elaine. *Hystories: Hysterical Epidemics and Modern Culture*. London: Picador, 1997.

————. *Sexual Anarchy: Gender and Culture at the Fin de Siecle*. New York: Viking, 1990.

Spiegelman, Art, and Bob Schneider, eds. *Whole Grains: A Book of Quotations*. New York: Douglas Links, 1973.

Stott, Carole. *Celestial Charts: Antique Maps of the Heavens*. London: Studio Editions, 1991.

Thompson, Damian. *The End of Time: Faith and Fear in the Shadow of the Millennium*. Sinclair-Stevenson, 1996.

Thurow, Lester C. *The Future of Capitalism: How Today's Economic Forces Shape Tomorrow's World*. New York: Morrow, 1996.

Toulmin, Stephen. *Cosmopolis: The Hidden Agenda of Modernity*. New York: The Free Press, 1990.

Tristram, Philippa. *Figures of Life and Death in Medieval English Literature*. London: Paul Elek, 1976.

Turner, Alice K. *The History of Hell*. Orlando, FL: Harcourt, Brace & Company, 1993.

Wagar, W. Warren. *Terminal Visions: The Literature of Last Things*. Bloomington: Indiana University Press, 1982.

Waldrop, M. Mitchell. *Complexity: The Emerging Science at the Edge of Order and Chaos*. New York: Simon & Schuster, 1992.

Weil, Andrew. *Spontaneous Healing: How to Discover and Enhance Your Body's Natural Ability to Maintain and Heal Itself*. New York: Knopf, 1995.

Weinberg, Steven. *Dreams of a Final Theory*. New York: Pantheon Books, 1992.

Whitfield, Peter. *The Image of the World: 20 Centuries of World Maps*. London: The British Library, 1994.

Wilson, Edward O. *The Diversity of Life*. Cambridge, MA: Belknap Press of Harvard University Press, 1992

Whole Earth. *The Fringes of Reason*. New York: Harmony Books, 1989.

Whole Earth. *The Millennium Whole Earth Catalog: Access to Tools and Ideas for the Twenty-First Century*. San Francisco: HarperSanFrancisco, 1994.

Wills, Christopher. *Plagues: Their Origin, History and Future*. New York: HarperCollins, 1996.

SOURCES

x. "This is written in the dark days ...":
Sacheverell Sitwell, *Sacred and Profane Love*
(London: Faber and Faber, 1940), p. 3.

xii. "But I told you when I began ...": William
Gibson, unpublished speech, given 1999.

6. "One by one the bulbs burned out ...": John
Crowley, *Little, Big* (Bantam, 1981), p. 538.

8. "Methinks the look of the world's ...": Thomas
Lovell Beddoes, *Death's Jest-Book; or, The Fool's
Tragedy* (written 1825; published anonymously
1850).

9. "O Judgment, thou art fled ...": William
Shakespeare, *Julius Caesar*, act 3, scene 2.

10. "We want the world to be a sacred part ...":
"The Politics of Storytelling," *Northern Lights*
(1994), eds. Deborah Clow and Donald Snow.

11. "In the vast interweaving of stories ...":
Allucquére Rosanne Stone, "Preface," in Timothy
Druckrey, ed., *Electronic Culture: Technology and
Visual Representation* (Aperture, 1996), pp. 7–8.

12. "If the silent, half-conscious, intuitive faith ...":
Henry Adams, *The Degradation of the Democratic
Dogma* (New York: Macmillan, 1919), pp. 246–47.

13. "Not I, not I, but the wind ...": D. H. Lawrence,
"Song of a Man Who Has Come Through," *The
Complete Poems of D. H. Lawrence*, eds. Vivian de
Sola Pinto and F. Warren Roberts (Viking, 1971).

14. "The engines of the end are spinning ...": *The
Little Book of Aphorisms of the End*, privately
issued, undated, unpaginated.

15. "You can see it in the movies ...": Chester
Lester, "Goin' by the Book," on *The Mystery of Life*
(Mercury Records, 1990–1991).

16. "There's flies in the kitchen ...": John Prine,
"Angel from Montgomery," on *John Prine* (Atlantic,
1971), credit: Cotillion-Sour Grapes, BMI.

18. "A nasty wind was blowing ...": Neil Young,
"Trans Am," on *Sleeps with Angels* (Reprise,
1994), credit: Silver Fiddle Music (ASCAP).

19. "When mankind shall again enjoy ...":
Heinrich Heine, *Scintillations* (New York: Henry
Holt, 1873), p. 159.

21. "Say to the children of Daniel Boone ...": *Little
Book of Aphorisms of the End*, privately issued,
undated, unpaginated.

22. "Things are more like they are now ...": Dwight
D. Eisenhower.

24. "The implicit message of the Smithsonian exhibition ...": Martin Palmer, *Dancing to Armageddon*
(Aquarian, 1992), p. 29.

25. "The hope that man might control the course
of events ...": Roderick Seidenberg, *Post-Historic
Man: An Inquiry* (University of North Carolina
Press, 1950), p. 228.

28. "Einstein spilled the beans.": *The Little
Book of Aphorisms of the End*, privately issued,
undated, unpaginated.

29. "If God did not exist ...": Voltaire, *Letters*.

30. "For within the hollow crown ...": William
Shakespeare, *King Richard the Second*, act 3,
scene 2.

32. "Behold, then, rising now, ...": William Gilpin,
quoted in *The West* by Bayrd Still (Capricorn,
1961).

33. "In the summer of 1976 ...": Stephen King, *The
Dead Zone* (Viking, 1979), pp. 413–14.

36. "Everybody knows that the boat is leaking....":
Leonard Cohen, "Everybody Knows," from
Stranger Music: Selected Poems and Songs
(Random House, 1993), copyright Leonard Cohen
and Leonard Cohen Stranger Music, Inc.

37. "'My friend,' said the orator, 'do you believe ...'":
Voltaire, *Candide*.

38. "We have reason to be afraid. ...": John
Berryman, quoted in Art Spiegelman and Bob
Schneider, eds., *Whole Grains: A Book of
Quotations* (Douglas Links, 1973), without source.

39. "Well, the last thing I remember...": Bob Dylan,
"Señor (Tales of Yankee Power)," on *Street Legal*
(Special Rider Music, 1978).

39. "But the possibility exists ...": J. Popper,
"Whoops," on Blues Traveler: *Save His Soul* (1993),
credit: Blues Traveler Pub. Corp., admin. by Irving
Music, Inc., BMI.

41. "Warlords of sorrow and queens …": Bob Dylan, "No Time to Think," on *Street Legal* (Special Rider Music, 1978).

42. "The real problem with theories of millenarianism …": Damian Thompson, *The End of Time: Faith and Fear in the Shadow of the Millennium* (Sinclair-Stevenson, 1996), p. xiv.

43. "Anti-Christ will have been born upon Midsummer Night.…": Sacheverell Sitwell, "The Birth of Anti-Christ," from *Splendours and Miseries* (Faber, 1943), p. 67.

44. "The moment had come …": Tom Lehrer, "In Old Mexico," from *An Evening Wasted with Tom Lehrer* (Reprise RS–6199), as reprinted in *Too Many Songs by Tom Lehrer* (Eyre Methuen, 1981), pp. 72–73.

46. "Then I had another dream,…": T. H. White, *The Book of Merlyn* (Austin: University of Texas Press, 1977), written circa 1940, p. 3.

46. "'The world of human society,' Vico wrote,…": Fernando Cervantes, *The Devil in the New World: The Impact of Diabolism in New Spain* (Yale University Press, 1994), pp. 154-55.

47. "I have set as my goal …": Jane Wagner, *The Search for Signs of Intelligent Life in the Universe* (Harpers, 1986), p. 98.

49. "'Well, you're not going to use the story, Mr. Scott?'…": Willis Goldbeck and James Warner Bellah from a story by Dorothy M. Johnson, *The Man Who Shot Liberty Valance* (1962), dir. John Ford.

51. "When we turn on the radio in a New York hotel …": William Gibson, unpublished speech.

53. "Death is psychosomatic.": Charles Manson.

54. "So if the question here is …": W. J. T. Mitchell, *The Last Dinosaur Book* (The University of Chicago Press, 1998), pp. 261–62.

59. "The breast is shut." *The Little Book of Aphorisms of the End*, privately issued, undated, unpaginated.

59. "The whole universe is balanced …": Joan Aiken, *The Cockatrice Boys* (Tor, 1996), p. 216

60. "And I lift my glass to the Awful Truth…": Leonard Cohen, "Closing Time," from *Stranger Music: Selected Poems and Songs* (Random House, 1993), copyright Leonard Cohen and Leonard Cohen Stranger Music, Inc.

62. "Look sometimes on the darker side of things.": Sundial motto, transcribed by John Parmenter in 1625.

62. "America was tired …": Eric Harrison, *Los Angeles Times* op-ed piece quoted in *The Guardian*, 18 May 1999.

65. "Slowly the poison the whole blood stream fills. …": William Empson, "Missing Dates," from *The Gathering Storm* (Faber, 1940).

66. "To build, brother, one has to build,…": Andrey Biely, *The Silver Dove* (1910; translation by George Greavey, Grove Press, 1974).

72. "Some years later, I met Maurice …": Peter Lennon, "A Kind of Joy," in the Weekend section of *The Guardian*, 2 May 1998.

73. "Everywhere in the world today …": *The Little Book of Aphorisms of the End*, privately issued, undated, unpaginated.

74. "The image of an end of time, …": Martin Palmer, *Dancing to Armageddon* (Aquarian, 1992), p. 56.

78. "Do you know what the great drama is?…": Oscar Wilde, in conversation with André Gide.

80. "Once upon a time there was a man …": Philip E. Slater, *The Pursuit of Loneliness: American Culture at the Breaking Point* (Beacon Press, 1970), pp. xi–xii.

87. "The Cities send to one another saying …": William Blake, *Vala, or the Four Zoas.*

92. "Order demands order.": Roderick Seidenberg, *Post-Historic Man: An Inquiry* (University of North Carolina Press, 1950), p. 27.

94. "Because a cold rage seizes …": David Thomson, *The City of Dreadful Night.*

95. "How come? How come we're one …": Ray Bradbury, "The Affluence of Despair," *Wall Street Journal*, 3 April 1998.

96. "I went to the cupboard, I opened the door,...": Randall Jarrell, "Song: Not There," in *Selected Poems* (1955).

97. "The natural inheritance of everyone...": Henry James Sr., *Substance and Shadow* (1863), p. 75.

97. "Why howl ye so...": F. Carruthers Gould, *Wild Nature* (London, John Lane the Bodley Head, 1903), unpaginated.

97. "I see your face, in every place,...": Jackson C. Frank, "Carnival" on Bert Jansch, *Toy Balloon*, Cooking Vinyl (Cook CD 138, 1998), credit: Pattern Music.

98. "Many of us would much rather...": Martin Palmer, *Dancing to Armageddon* (Aquarian, 1992), p. 145.

99. "Printers finde by experience...": Samuel Butler, *Prose Observations.*

104. "If you wanted to get America destroyed,...": Pat Robertson, quoted in the *San Francisco Examiner*, 7 September 1986.

105. "When the United States switches...": Michael Ellison in *The Guardian*, 10 February 1999.

106. "I don't think the human species...": Edward O. Wilson, author of *Sociobiology*, in *The New York Times*, 14 March 1995.

107. "Sign here for a cut...": *The Little Book of Aphorisms of the End*, privately issued, undated, unpaginated.

109. "So why all this about Satanism and demons?...": Martin Palmer, *Dancing to Armageddon* (Aquarian, 1992), p. 40.

110. "I only wish *I* had such eyes,' the King remarked...": Lewis Carroll, *Through the Looking Glass* (Macmillan, 1963 ed.).

112. "'Boy,' says Coyote, 'am I sore.' ...": Thomas King, *Green Grass, Running Water* (Boston: Houghton Mifflin Company, 1993), p. 358.

114. "I keep coming back to its central conceit...": Mark Kingwell, *Dreams of Millennium* (Toronto: Viking, 1996), p. 14.

114. "I knew I had to keep myself tidy...": Diana,

Princess of Wales, on being asked about her premarital virginity.

115. "It was difficult to irritate Satan...": Mark Twain, *The Mysterious Stranger* (New York, Harpers, 1916), p. 140.

116. "'Sentimentalists,' says the PILGRIM's SCRIP...": George Meredith, *The Ordeal of Richard Feverel* (London, Chapman and Hall, 1859), vol. 2, p. 171.

117. "The premise of Timequake One...": Kurt Vonnegut, *Timequake* (G.P. Putnam's Sons, 1997), pp. xii–xiii.

118. "It is very difficult in most...": Martin Palmer, *Dancing to Armageddon* (Aquarian, 1992), p. 104.

120. "This is the basic conspiracy...": Jack Womack, letter to the author, 11 August 1996.

124. "In the book 'Finding' ...": Gary Ross in the *New York Times*, 6 May 1999; quoting Edward Hallowell.

125. "We never voted to inhabit...": *The Little Book of Aphorisms of the End*, privately issued, undated, unpaginated.

126. "I remember you...": W. S. Merwin, "Vixen," in *Vixen* (Alfred A. Knopf, 1996), p. 69.

126. "The carnivalesque marketplace...": Michael André Bernstein, *Bitter Carnival: Ressentiment and the Abject Hero* (Princeton University Press, 1992), pp. 23–24.

127. "The world is a chess-board. ...": Kit Kelvin, *Kernels* (1860).

129. "The old Northern faith contained...": Max Nordau, *Degeneration* (London: Heinemann, 1895), from the second German edition.

129. "Turning and turning in the rising gyre...": William Butler Yeats, "The Second Coming," in *Michael Robartes and the Dancer* (1921).

130. "But oh, beamish nephew, ...": Lewis Carroll, *The Hunting of the Snark* (1876), Fit III.

132. "And then to grapple ...": Thomas Hardy, "Channel Firing."

139. "When your Daemon is in charge ...": Rudyard Kipling, *Something of Myself* (London: Macmillan, 1937), chapter 8.

141. "As the licensed fool evolves into the Abject Hero ...": Michael André Bernstein, *Bitter Carnival: Ressentiment and the Abject Hero* (Princeton University Press, 1992), pp. 23–24.

143. "Humanity must perforce ...": William Shakespeare, *King Lear*, act 4, scene 2.

144. "We have seen during the late 1980s ...": David Nabarro, in charge of WHO's Roll Back Malaria project, quoted in *The Guardian*, 12 May 1999, p. 10.

148. "Living as we do in the closing year ...": Edward Bellamy, *Looking Backward: 2000-1887* (Boston: Ticknor and Company, 1888), p. iii.

149. "It *was* the spirit world ...": Tim O'Brien, *In the Lake of the Woods* (Houghton Mifflin, 1994), p. 203.

150. "We live, after all, in the aftermath ...": Adrian Searle, reviewing Rosalind E. Krauss, *The Picasso Papers* (Thames and Hudson, 1998), in *The Guardian*, 2 May 1998.

158. "Malaria! said Tweedledum ...": *The Little Book of Aphorisms of the End*, privately issued, undated, unpaginated.

158. "Yep, son, we have met the enemy ...": Walt Kelly, *Pogo* (Simon and Schuster, 1951).

158. "Come follow us, and smile ...": Thomas Lovell Beddoes, "Sibylla's Dirge," from *The Poems Posthumous and Collected* (1851).

159. "The sea of faith was once ...": Matthew Arnold, "Dover Beach."

161. "I lay in my bed in my house at dingy Hammersmith ...": William Morris, *News from Nowhere: or, an Epoch of Rest* (Boston, Roberts Brothers, 1890), pp. 277–78.

162. "The first thing you'll notice ...": Fred Pfeil, "Second Class Lecture, Senior Livesaving Course," unpublished.

166. "Come one then, cry'd Panurge,...": Rabelais, *Gargantua and Pantagruel*.

174. "I shit in your album,' said the Horseman.": *The Little Book of Aphorisms of the End*, privately issued, undated, unpaginated.

176. "In the last quarter of the twentieth century ...": Tom Robbins, *Still Life with Woodpecker* (Bantam, 1980).

177. "'So,' he said. 'You're what we'd call a survivalist?' ...": Stephen Baxter, *Moonseed* (London: HarperCollins, 1998), p. 78.

178. "Why is order so wonderful?...": Morse Peckham, *Man's Rage for Chaos: Biology, Behavior, and the Arts* (Chilton Books, 1965), p. 39.

179. "And when He broke the seventh seal,...": Revelation, 8:1.

180. "I think it may be fitting to treat ...": John Clute, "Pilgrim Award Speech" in *Look at the Evidence: Essays and Reviews* (Seattle, Serconia Press, 1996), pp. 9–10.

181. "Over the last few decades ...": John Clute, ibid., p. 11.

182. "Bambakias swallowed painfully ...": Bruce Sterling, *Distraction* (New York, Bantam, 1998), p. 182.

185. "I think that life would suddenly ...": Marcel Proust, in *L'Intransigeant*; quoted by Alain de Botton in the *New York Times*, 12 January 1999.

187. "The only pictures on the walls ...": Russell Hoban, *Mr. Rinyo-Clacton's Offer* (Jonathan Cape, 1998).

188. "The 15,000 or so Hopis ...": Robert McG. Thomas Jr., obituary of Thomas Banyacya in the *New York Times*, 15 February 1999.

188. "Life is a process of breaking down ...": Ken MacLeod, *The Cassini Division* (Orbit, 1998), p. 90.

189. "The mass of men lead lives of quiet desperation.": Henry David Thoreau.

192. "Wind, jolly huntsman, your neat ...": Thomas Dekker, *The Sun's Darling* (1632–34).

197. "Transgression of norms is ...": Mark Kingwell, *Dreams of Millennium: Report from a Culture on the Brink* (Toronto: Viking, 1996), p. 211.

200. "Vulture/When you come for the white rat …": Randall Jarrell, "The Woman at the Washington Zoo," in *The Woman at the Washington Zoo* (1960).

200. "If the confidence man …": Lewis Hyde, *Trickster Makes the World: Mischief, Myth, and Art* (1998), p. 11.

201. "THERE ARE NO SERVICES ON THIS ROUTE.": Art Spiegelman and Bob Schneider, eds., *Whole Grains: A Book of Quotations* (Douglas Links, 1973), without source.

202. "Wait a minute, says that GOD. …": Thomas King, *Green Grass, Running Water* (Boston: Houghton Mifflin Company, 1993), pp. 33–34.

203. "Everyone is in the best seat.": John Cage.

203. "So, instead of trying to dance …": Martin Palmer, *Dancing to Armageddon* (Aquarian, 1992), p. 184.

203. "Mistah Kurtz—he dead.": Joseph Conrad, "Heart of Darkness," (1899, *Blackwood's Magazine*); quote from story as published in *Youth: A Narrative; and Two Other Stories* (Blackwood, 1902), pp. 168–69.

204. "PARABOLA: Is there a need to purge …": Ursula K. Le Guin, interview published in *Parabola* 23, no. 1 (February 1998), p. 23.

204. "In the desert I saw a creature, …": Stephen Crane, poem III, *The Black Riders and Other Lines* (1894).

206. "And God said unto Noah …": Genesis 6:13, 7:4.

207. "Life's a long tragedy, this globe's …": Isaac Watts, *Epistle to Mitio*, circa 1748.

207. "The Flood as we know it …": Norman Cohn, *Noah's Flood: The Genesis Story in Western Thought* (New Haven, Yale University Press, 1996) discusses the Mesopotamian and the biblical stories of the Flood at length.

208. "Alas for these latter days! …": Mary Shelley, *The Last Man* (1831).

210. "I saw four angels standing …": Revelation 7:1–3.

210. "My son has been a subscriber …": letter in the April 1989 *BBC Wildlife* magazine, as quoted by Martin Palmer in *Dancing to Armageddon* (Aquarian, 1992), p. 63.

211. "One world at a time.": Henry David Thoreau, in conversation.

212. "The grave's a fine and pleasant place …": Andrew Marvell, "To His Coy Mistress."

212. "And did those feet in ancient time …": William Blake, "A New Jerusalem," in *The Complete Poetry and Prose of William Blake* (University of California Press, 1982).

215. "They wept for humanity …": E. M. Forster, "The Machine Stops" (1909).

215. "Something like 40% more time behind the wheel …": report in *The Guardian*, 9 May 1999.

224. "Out of mist, God's …": Robert Penn Warren, "Interjection #6: What You Sometimes Feel on Your Face at Night" (complete poem), in *Or Else* (Random House, 1974), p. 66.

224. "Hunt, hunt again. If you do not …": Robert Penn Warren, "Treasure Hunt" (complete poem), in *Incarnations* (Random House, 1968), p. 10.

225. "Time does not repair. …": *The Little Book of Aphorisms of the End*, privately issued, undated, unpaginated.

227. "A wind rose, and a wind fell, …": Amy Lowell, "The Day That Was That Day," in *East Wind* (1926).

227. "I sate myself down for some time …": Edward Bulwer Lytton, *The Coming Race*, (Edinburgh, William Blackwood, 1871), p. 291.

227. "Ho! Eve! my grey carrion wife …": Thomas Lovell Beddoes, "The Song that Wolfram Heard in Hell" from *Death's Jest-Book; or, The Fool's Tragedy* (written 1825; published anonymously 1850).

228. "I mean, after all; you have to consider …": Philip K. Dick, *The Three Stigmata of Palmer Eldritch* (Doubleday, 1965).

227. "Over! Over! and that is the end of all stories.": Hans Christian Andersen, "The Fir-Tree."

SOURCES

COPYRIGHT ACKNOWLEDGMENTS

Palmer, Martin. *Dancing to Armageddon.*
Aquarian, 1992. Reprinted by permission of
HarperCollins *Publishers*, Inc.

Popper, John. Words from the song "Whoops."
© 1992 Irving Music Inc/Blues Traveler Publishing
Corp., USA. Rondor Music (London) Ltd, SW6 4TW.
Reproduced by permission of IMP Ltd.

Prine, John. Words from the song "Angel from
Montgomery." © Cotillion Music Inc., USA.
Warner/Chappell Music Ltd, London, W6 8BS.
Reproduced by permission of IMP Ltd.

Robbins, Tom. *Still Life with Woodpecker.*
Copyright © 1980 by Tom Robbins. Used by
permission of Bantam Books, a division of Bantam
Doubleday Dell Publishing Group, Inc.

Sitwell, Sacheverell. "The Birth of Anti-Christ,"
from *Splendours and Miseries.* Faber, 1943.
Reprinted by permission of David Higham
Associates.

Sitwell, Sacheverell. *Sacred and Profane Love.*
Faber, 1940. Reprinted by permission of David
Higham Associates.

Slater, Phillip E. *The Pursuit of Loneliness.* © 1970,
1976 by Phillip E. Slater. Reprinted by permission
of Beacon Press, Boston.

Vonnegut, Kurt. *Timequake.* Copyright © 1997 by
Kurt Vonnegut. Used by permission of G. P.
Putnam's Sons, a division of Penguin Putnam, Inc.

Wagner, Jane. *The Search for Signs of Intelligent
Life in the Universe.* Copyright © 1986 by Jane
Wagner Inc. Reprinted by permission of
HarperCollins*Publishers*, Inc. and Jane Wagner
Inc.

White, T.H. *The Book of Merlyn* . © 1977. Reprinted
by permission of the University of Texas Press.

Yeats, William Butler. "The Second Coming."
Reprinted with permission of Scribner, a division of
Simon & Schuster Inc., from The Collected Works
of W. B. Yeats: Vol. 1: The Poems, revised, Richard
J. Finnerann, Editor. (New York: Scribner, a
Division of Simon & Schuster Inc., 1989).